PENSTEMONS

Audrey Cooper

1st edition published January 1996

ISBN 1-898073-09-0

Acknowledgements
I would like to thank my husband Stan for all the initial
typing and editing. Ashwood Nurseries, Kings Winford for
their original help and enthusiasm. The Ladies of the
Lymington Hants Library for their patience and helpfulness
in obtaining all the reference books I needed. Mike Power
for his general guidance and advice. Grateful
acknowledgement to the Trustees of the Royal Gardens
Kew. The Royal Horticultural Society, Wisley for their help
and much correspondence. Mr P. Hares of the Special Plant
Unit, Pershore College of Horticulture.

Publisher's Note
Whilst every care has been taken to ensure the accuracy of
all the information given in this book neither the author nor
the publisher can accept responsibility for any mistakes that
may occur.

Power Publications
1 Clayford Ave
Ferndown, Dorset

Printed by: Pardy & Son (Printers) Ltd.
Edited by: Mike Power
Book photos: Mike Power and Barry Rickman
Design: Graham Whiteman
Cover photograph: Mike Power

Contents

$\mathscr{P}$enstemons

BEARDS TONGUE

The Penstemon is a very beautiful and versatile flower that will fit happily into almost any garden large or small. They are outstanding in any large herbaceous border, especially if inter-planted with gladioli or roses. The smaller species are highly suitable for the rock or scree garden, as their heights range from just a few inches to almost four feet.

The name Penstemon is derived from the Greek *Pent* - meaning five, and *Stemon* - a stamen - referring to the prominent sterile fifth stamen, but in the early garden reference books they were referred to as PENSTEMON. They are a member of the snap dragon family - *Scrophulariaceae*

In the early to mid-eighteenth century many large and very stately homes sent plant hunters to scour the world for rare and exotic plants to fill their 'stove houses'. It was very much a case of one-up-manship as to who acquired the very first unknown specimen, East - West no journey was too long or hazardous or, for that matter, too expensive. As early as 1750 penstemons were gradually coming into Great Britain.

Penstemons were first discovered growing in the wild along the west coast of America but later it was found that they grew in various climatic conditions including baking deserts and snow capped mountains roughly in a line extending from Alaska to Guatemala, one species even being found in Kamchatka, Japan. Further varieties were found as the wagon trains and the railways opened up the Americas.

As today, new plants and seeds, wherever they are discovered in the world, still have to survive journeys back to plant specialists for expert cultivation, but in the eighteenth and nineteenth centuries plant hunters did not have the benefit of modern packing and freezing facilities or the speed in transit, and in consequence, many plant specimens succumbed to the harsh conditions. In earlier times the discovery of new plants also meant that they had to survive a long and dangerous passage by horseback and pack mules, being manhandled through swamps, rivers and hostile Indian country etc., before starting the harrowing voyage around Cape Horn and across the Atlantic Ocean in sailing ships with all the dangers this entailed, a sea voyage which could last up to eight months or even longer.

In the mid-ninteenth century as further discoveries were made many new Penstemons started to appear.

The red flowered *P.hartwegii* from Mexico in 1825, the blue flowered *P.cobaea* coming from Nebraska and Texas. These seem to have been used as the basis for many of today's cultivars. Others were *P.hairtsutus*, *P.laevigatus*, *P.roezii*, *P.barbatus*, *P.campanulatus*, and *P.scouleri* etc..

P. George Holme

Flamingo

All bore the familiar tube shaped flowers, but their leaves varied in length, width, and various shades of green, some also had a variation in stem colour.

Diversity of natural habit gives a variety of tolerance to differing garden sites. The majority of commonly cultivated species i.e. *P.barbatus, P.isophyllus, P.hartwegii* are found in dry sunny sites or in sub-alpine woodland meadows and plains on light, often impoverished soils. Species such as *P.centranthifolius* are found in desert and semi-desert conditions. These are the least demanding in cultivations and are most frequently used in cold areas as annuals for seasonal colour, or where winter temperatures do not fall much below 5 degrees centigrade, and are planted out in herbaceous and mixed borders where they are usually found to be fairly drought tolerant. They are sometimes naturalized in an alpine flower lawn or wild garden.

From probably the two parent species *P.hartwegii* and *P.cobaea* have evolved the garden hybrids which are more frequently encountered in Great Britain than North America. A second group includes species such as *P.davidsonii, P.menziessii, P.scouleri, P.newberryi, P.acaulis,* and *P.rupicola,* which are all low growing small shrubs or mat forming plants of mountain areas. These may be grown in rock gardens, border fronts or scree gardens.

The greatest enemies of the genus in cultivation are frost and damp during the winter months. Species most resistant to frost and damp include *p. barbatus, p. ovatus, p. acuminatus, p. angustifolius, p. confertus, p .deffusus, p.digitalis, p.fruticosus, p.glaber, p.grandiflorus, p.hirsutus, p.laevitatus* and *p.menziesii.*

In 1920 the Royal Horticultural Society at Wisley reported on a trial of 190 cultivars and their expert knowledge and cultivation produced a remarkable change in the Penstemon giving it a more robust nature and a larger flower, combined with beautiful new colour shades. their seeds then become available. However, there seems to be a lot of confusion over the different names given to a single plant depending, in some instances, from which part of the country you lived and the soil conditions. The Royal Horticultural Society therefore in their wisdom collected flowers from different areas of the country and identified them e.g. Snow Storm, Royal White or Burford White. There will always be a slight confusion over names, partly due to the raising of the new cultivars and seeds which do not always come true.

A great deal of the credit for the successful cultivation of the Penstemon varieties as they are known today must be attributed to Forbes of Hawick, who after several years of cultivation and experimentation reported in the early twentieth century the successful rearing of about 120 different cultivars. It was due largely to their work in breeding that the species quickly improved. They were responsible for creating new cultivars, many of which carried their own name. In 1938 Forbes, kings of the Penstemon at the time, were offering for sale a general collection of Penstemons from 1/6d (12½p) to 2.6d (22½p) each or a selection from 10/6d (52½p) to 30 shillings (£1.50) per dozen.

Further trials by the Royal Horticultural Society between the years of 1991 and 1993 of approximately forty Penstemons resulted in over half of them being awarded a 'Certificate of Merit' for their robust nature and all round excellence in colour, resulting in a very fine set of cultivars. For your interest I have indicated those receiving the award in the following pages.

But, of course, cross pollination is being tried all the time so, by the time this book is finished there will, no doubt be a few more variations. I find, however that if Penstemons are grown in clumps in your garden bees have their own ideas and cross pollinated at will.

cross breeding of the original species has evolved many of today's large healthier cultivars. All Penstemons are hardy or half hardy but they are not a long lived plant, three to five years giving their best display of flowers in the second year. This is why it is always advisable to take cuttings to keep a regular supply of young plants to fill in where age or heavy frost has cut them down.

Cultivation

The Penstemon will thrive in any well drained soil if each year in the Spring some kind of fertilizer is added, either organic or any type of general fertilizer. They like a nice sunny position but will, I find, tolerate a little shade. Keep them on the dry side as they do not like getting their feet or crown wet. When a flower spike has dropped all its blooms, cut it down to where you can see new shoots this will help to extend the flowering season from June until late October, or until the first frosts, when the plant will then die back.

Mulch around the Penstemons with garden compost, leaf mould, or well rotted straw based manure. This will increase the fertility of the soil and help strengthen plant growth. In April tidy the plants up by cutting off any old stems from the previous year's growth which were left to help provide some protection during the winter months, being careful not to damage any of the new seasons growth which should be appearing.

Generally, in the Southern Counties of England the Penstemons will be fairly frost hardy, but some of the smaller more delicate varieties may need covering with peat or its equivalent, bracken, a large flower pot, or even a cardboard box will do, but remember to expose them to the light during the day. Having said that, it is always advisable to take a few cuttings as an extra precaution.

THE RULE OF THUMB IS THE NARROWER THE LEAF, THE MORE HARDY THE PLANT.

Taking Cuttings

Cuttings can be taken in September from strong side shoots about four inches long. Cut below a node or leaf joint, trim off the lower leaves, dip in hormone rooting powder and place in a pot filled with compost made from equal parts peat or its equivalent, coarse sand and vermiculite. It is important to gently water the cuttings before covering pots with a clear plastic bag. Use three short canes to keep the bag away from the cuttings and stretch an elastic band around the pot to complete the seal. Pots can then be placed in a greenhouse, cold frame or even on a kitchen window sill, but remember that ventilation should be given on warm sunny days.

If the cuttings are placed in a cold frame it is advisable to cover the frame with old matting or a similar material on frosty nights. The cuttings should be well rooted after approximately four weeks, and can be transferred into 4" pots and hardened off outside in the milder weather of late May or early June.

Purple Bedder

PLANTING OUT

Plant the larger species of Penstemon about 24" apart, not forgetting to water them in, but planting 12" apart will suffice for the smaller lower growing varieties. Your plants should flower in the first year, but by the second year you should have beautiful flowering plants and the time and trouble spent will be well rewarded.

Remember to keep dead heading as this will help to ensure a beautiful display of their wide range of colour throughout the season.

COLOURS

One of the outstanding features of the Penstemon is its wide range of beautiful colours from the deepest red, through all the pinks to almost pure white. From silvery delicate blue to deep purple with a combination of yellows thrown in for good measure. Many of these colours share their lovely hues with whites or creams in the flower throats, or on the flower petals, inside and out.

PENSTEMONS FROM SEED

Penstemons can, of course, be grown from seed which can be purchased from most good seed merchants. Care should be taken to follow carefully the growing instructions on the packet. Seeds give a nice display of bedding Penstemons but unfortunately true cultivars as listed in this book cannot be guaranteed.

FLOWER ARRANGEMENTS

The Penstemon flowers which appears loosely along a tall graceful stem fit elegantly with foliage and other flowers. Pick the stem when most of the tubular flowers are open and strip away any foliage that is likely to be under the water. Stand the flower stems in deep fresh water for about three hours before arranging.

Penstemons growing in the author's garden

Preserving Penstemons

The complete flowering stem cannot be preserved. Single flowers can, however, be removed from the growing stem and dried individually in desiccant, or placed between sheets of paper and pressed taking care to arrange them in such a way that their best profile is obtained.

Penstemons as Pot Plants

Penstemons make good pot plants for summer decoration of an unheated greenhouse, the varieties with smaller flowers being preferable to the large flowered ones. If wanted for this purpose they should be re-potted in April, in 5" pots, instead of being planted outdoors. The cooler they are kept the better, so it is as well to leave them in a cold frame, fully exposed to the air, until the flower buds begin to show.

There are two types of bedding, or florist's Penstemon - the large flowered and the small flowered varieties. The former are far more numerous than the latter.

Naming of Penstemons

The reader may sometimes wonder how some Penstemons got their names. Often they were named after their discoverers, or their family or friends, but perhaps, more often named after the likeness of the flower head or flower form, or perhaps after the place where it was originally found, or just named because of a person's own preference.

A case in point was Mr Ron Sidwell, a friend of Pershore Horticultural College, who lived at Ashton Under Hill, but who recently sadly passed away aged in his early nineties.

I am pleased to record his Penstemon successes i.e. Raven, Osprey, Blackbird, Whitethroat and Flamingo, all named after birds, probably just because he liked birds.

PENSTEMON FLOWERS

Penstemon flowers are divided into three sections, the tube at the base being the narrowest part widening into the main part of the flower, the throat and the lobe on which there are five petals, two on the upper and three petals on the lower throat. The stamen, situated on the corolla, turns upwards across the roof of the throat thus the top of the birds beak or the back of the insect is exposed to the pollen cells where the anthers and the stigma facilitate the transfer of the pollen to the raiders in their search for nectar. When the wasps or bees enter the flower throat they instinctively follow the "bee line" which helps direct their proboscis or tongue to the nectar through the maze of filaments coming out of the tube. Large headed bees with short tongues cannot reach all of the nectar thus the flower keeps its main stock for its regular customers as a reward for pollinisation.

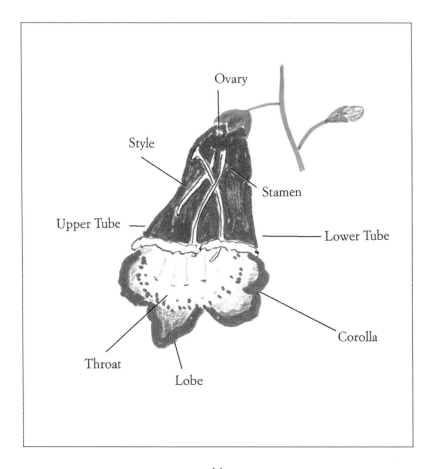

Where the Royal Horticultural Society as Wisley awarded a Certificate of Garden Merit in their trials during 1991-93 this is indicated against each flower by the letters A.G.M.)

P. "ALICE HINDLEY" (A.G.M.)
Raised by Forbes of Hawick in 1931. Height approximately 4ft (120cm). Tall erect type plant, might need some form of support. The only large pale mauve flower with an open white throat, upper corolla lilac fading to white in lower tube. Flowers from mid-July. Very showy summer plant that will need frost protection in the winter if temperature falls below freezing. One of the few penstemons that does not need too much pruning. (COMPARE WITH COUNTESS OF DALKEITH)

P. alluviorum
Medium to tall woody stemmed plant 3ft (80cm). Medium to broad lance shaped leaves carried on reddish stems. Prolific pale pink to white flowers, flowering in May-June. Likes moist soil in full sun. Needs frost protection. Native of Indiana, Illinois to Missouri, and south to Mississippi and Arkansas. Found by Pennell.

P. "APPLE BLOSSOM" (A.G.M.)
Medium height - 3ft (80cm). Bushy clump forming plant with pale pink delicate flowers tinged white and purple in throat. Dense narrow foliage, very prolific flowerer. Highly recommended. Half hardy but will need some protection in winter, especially in northern counties. (COMPARE WITH EVELYN)

P. baccharifolius
Medium height 2ft.(60cm). Plant shrubby at base with thick mid to dark green lance shaped leaves carried on red stems. Flowers deep pink to red in June-July. Likes dry soil and full sun. Half hardy but will need frost protection. Native of Texas and Mexico. Found by Hook.

P. " BLACKBIRD"
Tall willowy plant 4ft (120cm.) Deep red purple flowers, red streaks in narrow throat, stems dark red, elongated oval leaves. Plant will need some support. Half hardy, needs some protection in winter. (Compare with Burgundy)

P. Alice Hindley

P. "Beech Park" (Barbara Barker) (A.G.M.)
Medium height 2ft (60cm.) Large bright pink and white flowers inclined to
fade. No marks in open white throat, good summer flowering variety.
Needs protection in winter, semi-frost hardy. Recommended.
(Compare with P Peace and P Thorn)

P. barbatus
Medium height 2'6" (80cm.) Mid-green leaves lance shaped. Flowers June
to October. Long cerise scarlet flowers attached by short stalks at equal
distance along the main stem. Prefers full sun, fairly frost hardy but will
benefit from some frost protection in Northern Counties. Native of
Colorado, Nevada and South to Mexico. Found in 1794.

P. "Burgundy"
Tall 4' (120cm.) Strong plant with reddish purple flowers, white throat
streaked with dark red carried on dark red stems, medium glossy green
leaves. Half hardy will need some protection against frosts in northern
counties.
(compare with Blackbird, Midnight, Purple Bedder and Russian River.)

P. "Beitenbrush Blue"
Height 3" (8cm.) Low spreading type of plant with dainty blue flowers
tinged with pink. Leaves very small oval mid to dark green with a hint of
red. Ideal for front of border, rock or scree gardens. Needs protection from
frost in winter in all areas.

P. campanulatus (roseus)
Height 2ft. (60cm.) Mid-green lance shaped leaves. Bell shaped flowers of
rosy purple but occasionally white. Flowers individually spread on main
stem. Frost hardy in Southern Counties but advisable to protect in counties
further north. Found in Mexico and Guatemala.

P. companulatus (kunthii)
Medium height 18" (45cm.) Dainty bell shaped dark red flowers with white
streaked throat. Narrow lance shaped pale green leaves. Very suitable for
front of border or rock garden. Needs frost protection. Native of Mexico.
Found by George Don.

P. "Catherine-De-La-Mare" (A.G.M.)
Low growing spreading habit type plant 18" (45cm.) Native of California.
Small blue to purple flowers tinged pink with shiny green   small, oval
shaped leaves carried on red stems. Recommended for rock gardens or front
of the border. Colour differs with soil types. Will need good frost
protection in winter, especially in northern counties. Named after the
daughter-in-law of the famous poet, Walter De La Mare.
(Compare with Margery Fish and Sylvia Buss)

Top: Beech Park above: Burgundy

P. centranthifolius (**SCARLET BUGLER**)
Tall upright plant with woody base, may need some staking. Pale grey/green lance to oval leaves. Deep pink to scarlet, elongated pendular flowers April-July. Likes dry soil in full sun. Native of California. (George Bentham)

P. "CHERRY RIPE" (A.G.M.)
Tall plant 3'6" (110cm.) Profuse elongated cherry-red flowers on strong thin stems. Throat streaked red and white merging at mouth. Only half hardy needs frost protection especially in northern counties.
(COMPARE WITH ISOPHYLLUS AND CONNIES PINK)

P. "CHARLES RUDD" (A.G.M.)
Medium height 2ft. (60cm.) Purple flower with white throat, compact bushy plant with mid-green oval shaped leaves. Only half hardy needs frost protection.

P. "CHESTER SCARLET" (A.G.M.) (SYN. DAZZLER)
Medium height plant 3ft. (90cm.) Bright scarlet red flowers, white throat, streaked with red. Large oval green lance shaped leaves. One of the more beautiful showy penstemons of vigorous growth, highly recommended but does need some winter protection against frost.
(COMPARE WITH FLAME, RED EMPORER, AND SOUVENIR D'ANDRE TORRES)

P. clutei
Height 42" (107cm.). Leaves mid to grey green with serrate edges. Open mouthed pink flowers with purple streaks, narrow at base. Prefers well drained soil in full sun, will need frost protection. Native of Arizona. Found by A Nelson.

P. cobeae
Very low growing plant 8" (20cm.) Medium purple or white flowers late May to September. Leaves oblong to lance shaped. Ideal for rock or scree gardens. Needs good protection from frost in all areas. Found Nebraska to Missouri and Arkansas south to Texas.

P. "CONNIES PINK" (A.G.M.)
Tall upright plant 4ft (120cm.), many branched main stem. Narrow deep rose pink flowers streaked, with red throat. Fine grey-green lance shaped leaves. Needs protection against frost. (COMPARE WITH ISOPHYLLUS AND CHERRY RIPE.)

P. "COUNTESS OF DALKEITH"
Tall erect plant 3'6" (100cm.) Large open deep purple flowers with open
white throat. Strong sturdy stems carrying long lance shaped leaves of mid-
green. Needs some winter frost protection.
(COMPARE WITH ALICE HINDLEY)

P. confertus
Height 2" (5cm.), low growing. Flowers of sulphur yellow in mid-summer.
Rosette type plant with slender stems with minute mid-green oval to lance
shaped leaves. Ideal for rock or scree gardens. Needs protection against
frost in all areas. Discovered by David Douglas in British Columbia to
Alberta, and from Montana and Oregon.

P. cordifolius
Height 40" (100cm.) Tall scanty foliage, pyramid type inclined to droop.
Will need staking. Produces dull scarlet flowers in early summer. Leaves
shiny dark green oval shaped. Half hardy, needs frost protection. Found in
California.

P.. davidsonii - praeteritus
Height 6" (15cm.) Leaves are very small grey/green, oval shaped and
leathery. Early flowering - ruby red flowers growing from leaf joints. Half
hardy but needs some protection in all areas. Trim after plant has finished
flowering.

P. digitalis (HUSKERS RED)
Very low growing habit with spikes, tendency to spread, throwing up red
flower stems up to one metre in height carrying flushed red to purple
flowers. Generally purple nectar guides in flower tube. Glossy reddish
green leaves oblong to lance shaped or narrowly triangular. There is also a
white variety (**Woodville White**) Half hardy will need some protection in
winter. Found by Thomas Nuttal. Maine to S.Dakota, South to Texas,
Alabama and Virginia.

P. "DRINKSTONE"
Medium height 2'6" (80cm.) Bushy plant with narrow mid-green glossy
leaves on purple stems. Many deep pink to red flowers, white throat
streaked with red. Will meed frost protection in winter.
(COMPARE WITH ANDENKEN, FRIEDRICH HAHN AND SCHOENHOLZERI.)

P. "EVELYN"   (A.G.M.)
Height short to medium 2 feet (60 cm.) Very bushy plant with fine dense
narrow light green foliage with a profusion of dainty pink flowers with a
white throat, probably one of the most hardy of all the penstemons. Highly
recommended. (COMPARE WITH PINK ENDURANCE)

P. "FIREBIRD" - SEE SCHOENHOLZERI   (A.G.M.)

P. "FLAME"
Medium height 3 feet (90 cm.) Bright red flowers, white throat, streaked
with red and carried on reddish stems. Large sparse shiny green leaves. Half
hardy, needs frost protection in winter.

P. "FLAMINGO"
Height 3" (92cm). Leaves mid to dark green fleshy leaves. Large bright
reddish-pink flowers with round open white mouth, slightly streaked with
red. Showy flower and recommended. Will need frost protection.

P. fruticosus.
Height 6 to 12 inches (15-30cm.) Leaves narrow, lance shaped to oval.
Flowers lavender blue to purple. Suitable for rock or scree gardens. Trim
after flowering in late summer. Needs frost protection in all areas. Found
from Washington to Oregon, east to Montana and Wyoming.

P. "GARNET"   (ANDENKEN AN FRIEDRICH HAHN)   (A.G.M.)
Medium height 3ft. (90 cm.) Compact bushy plant with narrow mid-green
lance shaped leaves. Profusion of many wine red flowers, white throated
and streaked with red. One of the most popular garden penstemons for its
long flowering period. Highly recommended. A little more frost hardy than
most, but will need protection against east winds. Pershore College of
Horticulture found during their trials that Garnet was the only penstemon to
survive the infamous winter of 1981-2.

P. "GEORGE HOLME"
Height 20 inches (51cm.). Fleshy mid green leaves carried on thick green
stems. Deep cerise pink tubed flowers with clear white throat, no markings.
Flowers in July-late August. Half hardy will need some frost protection.

P. gentianoides
Fine bushy plant. Small violet blue flowers with white throat.

P. glaber
Height 18" (46 cm.) Compact plant throwing up very dainty blue to purple
flowers from June to September. Very grey oval leaves veined in red. Needs
frost protection in all areas. Native of South Dakota to Nebraska, Wyoming
and Arizona.

Clockwise from top left: Evelyn, Firebird, Glaber and Garnet

P. gracilis
Small violet blue flowers with white throat. Broad serrate leaves - similar to
P. gentianoides.

P. hartwegii (A.G.M.) (SYN. TORQUAY GEM)
Medium height 2'6" (80 cm.) Elongated bright red flowers, white throat
streaked red hanging in pendular sprays. Leaves grey to mid-green, long and
slender on dark red stems. Needs support and protection in winter. First
found in Mexico. (COMPARE WITH WINDSOR RED)

P. hallii
Blue violet flowers, low growing habit.

P. hartwegii albus
Medium height 2'6" (80 cm.) Many pretty cream flowers with white throat
hanging in pendula sprays. Leaves grey to mid-green, long and slender.
Needs support and protection in winter. First found in Mexico.
(COMPARE WITH WHITE BEDDER)

P. heterophyllus (TRUE BLUE)
Height 10 ins. (25 cm.) Low growing matt forming bushy plant bearing
narrow lance shaped pale green leaves. Very pure blue tubular flowers
borne on side shoots. Suitable for rock or scree gardens, flowers from June
to August. Will need covering against frost. Found in California.
Slight variations in the above named plant i.e. Blue Eye, Blue Fountain, Blue
Gem and Blue Robin.

P. "HEWELL PINK BEDDER" (A.G.M.)
Medium height 2'6" (80 cm.) Loose clump forming plant, with bright red to
pink flowers with white throat streaked with red. Flat to oval grey-green
leaves on reddish-brown stems. Half hardy will need some winter protection.
(COMPARE WITH HIDCOTE PINK AND MODESTY)

P. "HIDCOTE PINK" (A.G.M.)
Tall upright plant 3'4" (100 cm.) Very many erect stems with pretty rose
pink flowers. Throat cream streaked with red on reddish stems. Leaves soft
grey-green, oval to lance shaped. Half hardy will need frost protection.
Hybrid raised at Hidcote. (COMPARE WITH HEWELL PINK BEDDER AND
MODESTY)

P. "HIDCOTE PURPLE"
Tall upright plant 3'4" (100 cm.) Very many erect stems with pretty lilac to
purple flowers. Throat cream streaked with purple on reddish stems.
Leaves soft green-grey, oval to lance shaped. Will benefit from frost
protection. (COMPARE WITH HIDCOTE PINK AND MODESTY)

Hidcote Pink

P. hirsutus
Medium erect plant 2'6" (80 cm.) Flowers dull purple with white lobes.
Leaves mid-green oblong to lance shaped. Flowers in late summer but will
need some protection from frost. First found in 1758 in Eastern North
America, Quebec and Maine to Michigan and Wisconsin, South to Virginia
and Kentucky.

P. "HOLLY"
Very low growing plant 5" (13 cm.). Small dark green holly shaped leaves
and dainty pale mauve flowers. Will need frost protection. Very suitable for
rock and scree gardens.

P. "HOPLEYS VARIEGATED"
Medium height plants 24" (61 cm.). Variegated gold and pale green lance
shaped leaves. Pretty purple flowers with white underside. Flower throat
white streaked with purple. Will need frost protection. A sport from
Burgundy, propagated by Hopleys Nurseries.

P. isophyllus (A.G.M.)
Tall slender plant 4ft. (120 cm.) Reddish pink long tubular flowers, cream
throat tinged with red. Leaves lance shaped, grey to mid-green. One
penstemons that does need support and has to be protected in very cold and
frosty weather. Native of Mexico, found by Robinson.
(COMPARE WITH CHERRY RIPE AND CONNIE'S PINK)

P. Jamesii
Height 24" (60 cm.). Long narrow lance shaped, mid-green leaves. Flowers
creamy white with darkish tinge and hairs in throat. Prefers well drained soil
in warm position. One of the more frost tolerant. Native of Colorado, Utah,
New Mexico and Arizona. Found by George Bentham.

P. "KING GEORGE V"
Medium height 3 ft. (90 cm.) Beautiful bright red flowers with white throat
streaked with red. Mid-green shiny oval to lance shaped leaves. Highly
recommended. Will need some protection from frost. Raised by Forbes of
Hawick in 1911. (COMPARE WITH MAURICE GIBBS AND RUBICUNDUS)

King George

Margery Fish

P. "Knightwick"
Broad leaves. Purple pink flowers with densely streaked throat.

P. aevigatus
Medium height 3ft. (90 cm.) Pale violet flowers with white to very pale lilac throat. Shiny green narrow lance shaped leaves. Will need some frost protection in winter. Found in Pennsylvania to Mississippi and Florida.

P. lyallii
Small amethyst blue flowers in dense clusters. Broad mid-green serrated leaves.

P. "Margery Fish" (A.G.M.)
Low growing plant 12ins. (30 cm.) Very shiny dark green leaves with reddish-green stems. Profusion of dainty blue to violet flowers. Highly recommended for the rock garden or front of border. Good strong growing plant that will need a little protection from heavy frosts.
(Compare with Catherine de la Mare)

P. "Maurice Gibbs" (A.G.M.)
Medium erect plant height 3ft. (90cm.) Large open showy purplish red flowers with clear white open throat. Mid-green shiny leaves. Needs a little frost protection. (Compare with King George and Rubicundus)

P. "MADAM GOLDING"

Medium growing plant 2ft. (60cm.) Leaves light to dark green. Very pretty deep coral-red flowers with strongly marked throat. Suitable for the back of the rock garden. Needs some frost protection.

P. "MERLIN"

Medium growing plant 2ft. (60cm.) Shiny dark green leaves. Beautiful deepest purple flowers. Suitable for the back of the rock garden and borders. Will need frost protection.

P. "MIDNIGHT"

Medium height plant 3ft. (90 cm.) Dense mid to dark green foliage. Deep indigo purple flowers with white throat, heavily streaked with reddish purple, borne on long red stems. Will need protection from frosts.
(COMPARE WITH BURGUNDY, PURPLE BEDDER AND RUSSIAN RIVER)

P. "MILLS PINK"

Medium height plant 24" (61 cm.). Medium broad green lance shaped leaves. Elongated deep pink flowers with white throat streaked with red. Strong growing plant but will need some frost protection in Northern Counties.

P. "MODESTY"

Medium height plant 2'6" (80 cm.) Olive green shiny leaves. Bright reddish pink flowers with white throat streaked deep red, borne on grey-green stems. Will need protection from frosts.
(COMPARE WITH HEWELL PINK BEDDER AND HIDCOTE PINK)

P. "MOTHER OF PEARL"

Tall erect plant 3'6" (110 cm) Delicate grey-green foliage. Profusion of small flowers pearly-cream tinged with pastel blue or lilac, white throat streaked with purple. Will need some protection against frosts.
(COMPARE WITH STAPLEFORD GEM AND SOUR GRAPES)

P. "MRS. M. B. MORSE"

Medium height 2ft. (60cm.) Narrow shiny dark green leaves. Profusion of tubular elongated bright red flowers, throat white streaked with red. Recommended but will need frost protection.

P. "MYDDLETON GEM"

Medium height 2'6" (75 cm.) Olive green leaves. Bright reddish pink flowers with white throat tinged with pink. Recommended. A very fine cultivar but needs frost protection.
(COMPARE WITH PENNINGTOM GEM AND SOUTHGATE GEM)

Top: Merlin, below Midnight

P. *newberryii*
Very low growing matt growing plant height 8in. (20cm.) Very small oval dark green shiny leaves. Bears short sprays of tubular deep rose pink flowers in mid-summer. Very suitable for rock or scree gardens. Trim back after flowering. Will need good frost protection. Found in California and Nevada.

P. "OAKLEY RED"
Medium height plant 24" (61 cm.). Very dark green lance shaped shiny leaves. Flowers dark crimson red with throat also streaked dark red. Strong growing plant but will need some frost protection in winter.

P. "OLD CANDY PINK"
Rose pink flowers with white streaked throat.

P. "OSPREY" (A.G.M.)
Tall loose clump forming plant height 3'6" (110 cm.) Medium to large shiny lance shaped leaves. Large stubby cream flowers, cream throat with pink lower lip. Very showy and recommended. Will need some protection against frost. (COMPARE WITH FLAMINGO)

P. *ovatus*
Medium to low growing plant 2ft. (60 cm.) Mid-green narrow shiny lance shaped leaves. Deep purple flowers with pale lilac throat. Suitable for rock

Oakley Red   *Osprey*

Papal Purple

garden or front of the border. Flowers June to September. Quite hardy but
some frost protection recommended. Found by David Douglas. Plant
native to British Columbia, Washington and North Oregon.

P. palmeri
Tall growing plant 47" (120 cm.). Narrow to lance shaped mid-green leaves.
Large open mouthed creamy pink flowers with purple streaks. Flowers
March to September. Likes dry well drained soil. Needs frost protection.
Native of California to S.Utah and Arizona. Found by A Gray.

P. "PAPAL PURPLE"
Very low growing plant height 12in. (30 cm.) Bright green narrow leaves.
Pale purple bell-like flowers, with white throat tinged with purple. Very
suitable mound forming plant for rock or scree gardens. Needs good frost
protection. Recommended.

P. "PEACE"
Medium growing plant 2ft (60 cm.) Lance shaped mid-green leaves. Dense
growing habit with pink and white flowers tipped with red. Open white
throat with no markings. Young buds tipped with red, fading on opening.
Will need frost protection.
(COMPARE WITH BEECH PARK AND THORN.)

P. "PENNINGTON GEM" (A.G.M.)
Tall growing plant 43" (110 cm.). Very bushy plant with mid to greyish green leaves growing opposite each other. Bright clear pink flowers, white throat streaked with a few deep purplish red lines.
(COMPARE WITH MYDDLETON GEM AND SOUTHGATE GEM.)

P. "PENROSE THOMAS"
Medium height 2ft. (60 cm.). Blue flowers with white throat streaked with purple. Very dull dark green large lance shaped leaves carried on reddish stems. Flowers from end of June. Will need frost protection in Northern Counties.

P. "PERSHORE PINK NECKLACE"
Height about 30" (76 cm.). Large mid-green fleshy lance shaped leaves. A beautiful new showy plant having large pink flowers with a deeper pink necklace around a white throat. Plant was raised from seed collected by Pershore College of Horticulture about two to three years ago. Believed to be a cross from Flamingo and at one time was almost thrown away.

P. "PHARE"
Medium height plant 32" (80 cm.). Mid-green lance shaped leaves. Elongated scarlet flowers carried on thin purple stems. White throat slightly flecked with red. Bushy habit.

P. procerus
Very low growing habit only 7in. (20 cm.) Deep purple magenta flowers and small dark shiny oval green leaves. Very suitable for rock or scree gardens. Needs good protection from frost in northern counties. Found by David Douglas, Alaska to Oregon, east to Wyoming and Colorado.

P. "PINK ENDURANCE"
Medium height 2'6" (70 cm.) Very many narrow dense lance pointed leaves. Profusion of dainty pink flowers very similar to "Evelyn" but a shade larger. One of the more hardy penstemons and well worth growing. Protect from east winds. Highly recommended.

P. pinifolius
Very low growing woody at base, approximately 6" (15 cm.) in height. Delightful little shrubby species throwing up spikes of orange-red tubular flowers. Spiky leaves crowded on lower part of stem. Suitable for rock or scree garden or front of border. Likes a warm dry sunny situation away from cold east winds. Will need frost protection. Found in New Mexico, Arizona and Mexico. (COMPARE WITH MERSEA YELLOW)

Pennington Gem

P. pinifolius ("MERSEA YELLOW")
Very low growing woody at base, approximately 6" (15 cm.) in height. Same delightful little shrub, similar in habit to P. PINIFOLIUS but with primrose yellow flowers. Suitable for rock or scree gardens or front of the border. Likes a warm dry sunny situation away from cold winds. Needs protection from frost in winter. Found in New Mexico to Arizona and Mexico. (COMPARE WITH P. *pinifolius*)

P. "PINK DRAGON"
Very low growing 6in. (15 cm.) Very delicate deep pink flowers on short stems. Leaves pale green to grey. Very suitable for rock or scree gardens. Will need protection from winter frosts.

P. "PORT WINE" (A.G.M.)
Tall elegant plant 40" (100 cm.). Mid-green lance shaped leaves. Elongated large red to purple flowers carried on reddish green stems. Throat streaked with purple. (COMPARE WITH RAVEN AND RICH RUBY.)

P. "PRAIRIE FIRE"
One of the tallest plants 60" (150 cm.). Leaves basal rosette forming long and lance shaped grey to dark green on red stems. Orange to red flowers with deep pink throat finely streaked with dark red.

P "PURPLE BEDDER"
Medium height 2'6" (90 cm.) Deep purple flowers with purple throat streaked with dark red. Mid-green oval to lance shaped shiny leaves. Strong stems purple to green, grows horizontal then vertical. Will need some support. Not frost hardy in northern counties.

P. "RAJAH"
Height 24" (61cm.). Bushy plant, leaves similar to Garnet, but flowers are a much darker red and more elongated, similar to Firebird. Flowers from July to October. Will need frost protection.

P. "RICH RUBY"
Tall erect plant 3ft. (90 cm.) Large ruby red to purple flowers, white throat heavily streaked dark red carried on strong reddish stems. Leaves oval to lance shaped are a leathery dark green. Frost hardy but will need some protection in northern counties.
(COMPARE WITH PORT WINE AND RAVEN)

P. "RAVEN" (A.G.M.)
Tall erect plant 3ft. (90 cm.) Large deep purple flowers, throat white streaked with dark reddish purple. Stems strong green tinged with reddish purple. Leaves large oval to lance shaped, tinged with purplish hue.
(COMPARE WITH PORT WINE AND RICH RUBY)

Opposite top left to right: Raven and Rich Ruby

P. "RED EMPEROR"
Medium height 2'6" (90 cm.) Large showy bright red flowers with white throat streaked dark red carried on red stems. Mid-green oval to lance shaped leaves.
(COMPARE WITH CHESTER SCARLET, FLAME, SOUVENIR-DE-ANDRE TORRES)

P. "RIDGEWAY RED"   (NEW)
Tall plant and vigorous grower. Large red flowers with slightly streaked throat.

P. rostriflorus
Height 42" (107 cm.). Very narrow long lance shaped leaves. Crimson elongated narrow red flowers carried on mid-green stems. Will need some frost protection. Likes well drained soil in full sun. Flowers May to September. Native of California, Arizona, Colorado to New Mexico. Found by Gray.

P. "ROY DAVIDSON"
Very low spreading plant 4" (12 cm.). Pale green narrow lance shaped leaves. Very dainty pale pink flowers with deeper pink base. Ideal for rock or scree gardens. Will need frost protection.

P. rubicundus   (A.G.M.) (SYN. HEYTHROP PARK)
Very tall erect plant 4ft. (120 cm.) Very large bright scarlet flowers with wide open white mouth, slightly streaked dark red. Dark green broad oval to lance shaped leaves. Flowers July to September. Hardy but a little protection from frost recommended in northern counties.
(COMPARE WITH KING GEORGE AND MAURICE GIBBS)

P. rupicola
Height 8in. (20 cm.) Forming flattened mats of blue grey fleshy small green leaves. Flowers deep rose pink carried on 10cm. stems. Ideal for rock or scree gardens. Flowers in spring to late summer. Will need good frost protection in northern counties. Also a lovely white version "Albus" Found Washington to California.

P. "RUSSIAN RIVER"
Medium height 2'6" (70 cm.) Deep purple to blue flowers, throat purple heavily streaked with red, carried on dark purplish stems. Leaves glossy dark green oval to lance shaped. Hardy but will need protection in northern counties.
(COMPARE WITH BURGUNDY, MIDNIGHT, AND PURPLE BEDDER)

P. roezlii (laetus)
Very low growing 6in. (15 cm.) Mat forming plant of bright green leaves.
· Flowers long and tubular with prominent lip in colours of dainty pink to lavender. Highly recommended for rock or scree gardens. Will need frost protection. Found by A Gray in 1782, Oregon to California and Nevada.

P. *serrulatus* (SYN. DIFFUSUS)
Height 24in (60 cm.) A cascade penstemon with broad flat oval dark green leaves. Stems carry clusters of deep blue to dark purple flowers. Will tolerate a little more moisture than most penstemons. There is also a white version, Albus. Hardy, but frost protection recommended in northern counties. Found south Alaska to Oregon.

P. scoulerii fruticosus
Low growing 6in. (15 cm.) Mat forming dense broad clumps, shrubby at base. Leaves narrow to lance shaped mid-green, often lustrous. Clusters of small purple flowers, long tubed with prominent lip. Suitable for rock or scree gardens. Also a white form Albus. Will need frost protection. Found by David Douglas - N.Washington to N. Idaho and British Columbia.

P. "SCHOENHOLZERI" (SYN "FIREBIRD") (A.G.M.)
Medium height 3ft. (90 cm.) Vigorous and upright, produces trumpet shaped brilliant scarlet flowers on reddish stems. Leaves mid-green, oval to lance shaped. Flowers from mid-summer to autumn. Recommended. Hardy but will need some protection in northern counties.
(COMPARE WITH GARNET (ANDENKEN AN FRIEDIRCH HAHN) AND DRINKSTONE.)

P. "SIX HILLS" (HYBRID) *(DAVIDSONII X PERIANTHERUS)*
Very low growing 6in. (15 cm.) Bushy habit bearing dainty rosy to violet flowers on short stems. Fleshy grey-green leaves. High suitable for rock or scree gardens. Flowers spring to late summer. Frost protection recommended.

P. "SNOWSTORM"

Medium height 2ft. (60 cm.) Beautiful large almost pure white flowers carried on pale green upright stems with shiny lance shaped mid-green leaves. Flowers from late June until late summer. Frost protection recommended in all areas. (COMPARE WITH WHITE BEDDER.)

P. "SOUR GRAPES"

Medium height 3ft. (90 cm.) Flowers deep purple with blue almost aluminium base. White throat finely streaked purplish red. Flowers grow in bunches along the stem, hence the name. Medium leaves mid to dark green, oval to lance shaped. Hardy but will need some protection in northern counties. (COMPARE WITH MOTHER OF PEARL AND STAPLEFORD GEM.)

Sour Grapes

Chester Scarlet

P. "SOUTHCOMBE PINK"
Pink flowers with white streaked throat.

P. "SOUTHGATE GEM"
Medium height 2'6" (75 cm.)   Flowers bright cherry red, white throat finely
streaked with red. Very dark green lance shaped leaves. Hardy but some
frost protection recommended.
(COMPARE WITH MYDDELTON GEM AND PENNINGTON GEM)

P. "SOUVENIR-D-ANDRE-TORRES"
Medium height 2'6" (75 cm.) Large bright scarlet flowers, white throat
streaked with red. Stems upright and very dark purplish red. Leaves oval to
lance shaped, dark green tinged with purple. Hardy but frost protection
recommended in northern counties.
(COMPARE WITH FLAME, CHESTER SCARLET AND RED EMPEROR)

P. "STAPLEFORD GEM" (A.G.M.)
Tall bushy plant 3'4" (100 cm.) Lilac to blue flowers, white throat streaked
purplish red. Very dense grey-green leaves, oval to lance shaped.
Recommended. Hardy but frost protection recommended in northern
counties. (Native of N.E. America, from Quebec, Ontario to Wisconsin,
Virginia, Kentucky and Tennessee)
(COMPARE WITH MOTHER OF PEARL AND SOUR GRAPES.)

P. strictus
Medium growing plant 24" (60 cm.). Deep green lance shaped leaves. Deep
violet to blue flowers having short fat tubes on tall spikes. Flowering June -
July. Needs frost protection. Native of South Wyoming and Utah, N.E.
Arizona to New Mexico.
Found by George Bentham.

P. superbus
Tall strong woody growing plant 48" (122 cm.). Oval grey green leaves.
Crimson flowers carried on red stems. Flowering April-May. Needs frost
protection. Likes well drained soil in full sun. Native of S.E. Arizona and
New Mexico.
Found by A Nelson.

P. "SUTTON'S PINK BEDDER"
Medium height 2'6" (80 cm.) Very dense compact bushy plant with shiny
mid-green foliage. Pale pink flowers with clear white throat. Hardy but
frost protection recommended in northern counties.
(COMPARE WITH WHITE THROAT)

P. "SYLVIA BUSS"
Low growing inclined to spread, height 18in (45 cm.) Very profuse mid-blue
to mauve flowers carried on reddish green stems. Leaves mid-green and
shiny. Bushy habit suitable for rock gardens. Will need some frost
protection in winter.

P. "TALL PINK" CULTIVAR YET TO BE NAMED
Medium height 80cm. Erect plant with grey-green foliage.
Dusty pink flowers with strong red tipped cream lower tube. Throat white
finely streaked with deep purplish red. (COMPARE WITH HIDCOTE PINK.)

P. "THORN"
Medium height 3ft (90 cm.) Small narrow elongated pink and white flowers
with white throat tending to fade with age. Long narrow dark green lance
shaped leaves with pale green stems. Bushy habit. Hardy but needs
protection in northern counties. (COMPARE WITH PEACE AND BEECH PARK)

P. "THREAVE PINK"
Dense narrow leaves. Small tubular reddish purple flowers with streaked
throat.

P. utahensis
Height 18" (46 cm.). Fleshy lance shaped grey-green leaves backed with
reddish hue. Flowers carmine pink carried on red stems similar to digitalis.
Flowering July to October. Will need frost protection.

P. venustus
Medium growing shrubby type plant 32" (80 cm.). Broad mid-green leaves
carried on reddish stems. Flowers lilac to purple, throat streaked with
purple. Flowering May to August. Needs frost protection and prefers full
sun. Native of Idaho, Washington and Oregon.
Found by D Douglas.

P. virgatus arizonicus

P. "WHITE BEDDER" (A.G.M.)
(SYN. ROYAL WHITE AND Burford White)
Medium height 2'6" (70 cm.) Abundance of large white flowers tinged with
pink especially on bud tips. Lance shaped narrow dark green leaves carried
on pale green stems. Flowers July onwards. Hardy except in northern
counties.
(COMPARE WITH SNOWSTORM, ROYAL WHITE AND BURFORD WHITE)

P. "WHITE THROAT"
Medium height 3ft.(90 cm.) Flowers deep reddish pink with clear white
throat with no markings. Good clump forming plant with medium green
lance shaped shiny leaves carried on pale green stems. Half hardy will need
frost protection.
(COMPARE WITH SUTTON PINK BEDDER)

P. watsonii
Low flowering 12in (30 cm.) Deep purple to violet, or white in part, narrow
funnel shaped flowers carried on 60 cm. stems. Oval to lance shaped dark
green leaves. Clump forming good spreader. Ideal for rock gardens.
Flowers in mid-summer. Half hardy will need frost protection.
Found by A Gray - Colorado, Utah and Nevada.

Snow Storm

P. whippleanus
Low growing 4in. (10 cm.) Dainty purple flowers in July and August. Occasionally shows cream flowers, carried on 17 cm. purplish green stems. Leaves large oval green blotched with purple. Very good spreader. Suitable for rock garden. Half hardy will need some frost protection. Found by A Gray. Native of Wyoming and Idaho, south to Colorado, Utah, New Mexico and Arizona.

P. "WINDSOR RED"   (SYN. COTTAGE GARDEN RED)
Medium height 2'6" (70 cm.) Very bushy plant with narrow mid-green leaves. Bright red elongated flowers with white throat with a few red streaks. Flowers carried on long fine reddish purple stems. Hardy but will need frost protection in northern counties. Recommended.
(COMPARE WITH P.HARTWEGII)

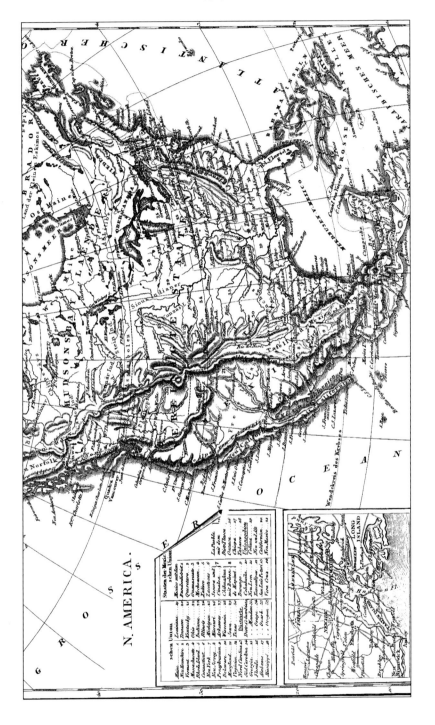

David Douglas F.H.S.
1798 to 1834

A short history of one of the most intrepid plant hunters of all time.

I make no apology for including in this book on penstemons a short history of David Douglas one of the most famous plant hunters. Perhaps when you have read it you will agree, and when in future, you look at a penstemon or many of the other flowers in your garden, they will hold that little bit extra mystique behind their beauty.

David Douglas was born in Scone, Perthshire, in 1798, the second son of a stone mason. He had his first practice in foot slogging, something that was to come in very handy with a daily journey of six miles to school and back at Kinnoul. Young David showed his metal early, being described as self-willed almost to obstinacy to his master and to his strap. His love of nature appeared early in his liking for fishing and bird nesting rather than school. He would bring home all manner of pets including birds, owls and hawks.

When he was about ten he left school to become a gardener's boy in the garden and nursery at the Earl of Mansfield's Scone Palace, where he was usually in trouble from his Master, Mr Beattie for many quarrels with the other Bothy boys. Young Douglas was a very quick learner for after only seven years at Scone Palace he was appointed first gardener in the kitchen garden. His Master Beattie then recommended him to Sir Robert Preston at Valley Field on the Firth of Forth, a garden noted for its fine collection of exotic plants.

Douglas joined the staff in 1818. Sir Robert realised the young gardener's worth and gave him the run of his extensive botanical and garden library. After two years Douglas then moved on to Glasgow Botanic Gardens under Professor William Hooker, himself a noted early plant hunter, who gave him a great deal of encouragement and took him to the Highlands to help him collect material for his books.

In the spring of 1823 William Hooker having been consulted by Joseph Sabine about a suitable person as a botanical collector to the Horticultural Society quickly recommended Douglas. At only 24 years of age he entered the service of a Society to which he was to bring almost incredible horticultural gains and honour.

Although Sir Joseph Banks wrote a letter to Kew that the salary for botanical travellers should be increased from £100 to £180 per year, the Society stuck to £100. So even in the 1820's Douglas was certainly not taking the position for the money, anyway he never seemed to have any.

His main job was to collect seeds as well as any specimens he might find that were not already growing in this country. John Lindley, gardens clerk at Chiswick, was in the process of drawing up a pamphlet for all the Society's collectors. There is no doubt Douglas found this invaluable, it told collectors that if they found wet seeds, to dry them thoroughly before wrapping in brown paper and placing in a bottle or similar vessel, before being placed in the driest part of the ship. Large fruit stones had to be cleaned of their pulp then placed in wet clay or mud. Cuttings of fruit trees had to be stuck in wet clay before being wrapped in wet moss.

Douglas was to be quickly despatched on his first mission and on June 3 1823 he left Charing Cross by coach for Liverpool and the United States of America. He arrived at Liverpool in the early morning only to be told his ship, the 'Ann Maria' would not be sailing for another day. He decided, therefore, to go off and study some American plants in the local botanic gardens. Next day he was back on board early in the morning bound for New York.

Initially they had to negotiate the River Mersey with four tugs pulling and eventually they sighted the Welsh mountains. Almost all were seasick at first, the weather being very rough. It was July before they sighted Newfoundland. In heavy seas and gale force winds, the treacherous weather kept following them, tearing at the ship's canvas and slowing them down until rations began to run low. The sailors even chewed their tobacco, dried it out and then smoked it in their pipes.

Douglas had spent so much of his money on equipment and nothing on clothes that when the ship docked at New York, he realised how awful he looked. He had to go and spend a sixpence or two on some clothes to make himself a little more presentable.

By September 8 he was on his way to Canada by stage coach to Utica, but after 70 miles on such a bad road he could stand the bumping and jostling no longer and was obliged to give it up and take a river boat. This suited him much better, so at a leisurely pace he now made for Rochester, some 60 miles away, where he changed to the stage coach again for Buffalo and Lake Erie. He reached there at midnight on September 12th. Next day he had to face another six hour journey by steamer to Amherstburg.

On September 16 he wrote in his diary "this is what I might term as my first day in America". The magnitude of the scenery, the trees and the rich black soil had really taken hold of him. He saw vast crops of Indian corn, rich flora and fauna that he could never have imagined.

Trouble, however, seemed to follow Douglas all of his life. On one occasion a French horse - which could not understand a word of English - took off with all his notes, seeds etc, in his jacket pocket, leaving him stranded up a tree. He managed to get himself rescued but, of course, all his precious information had disappeared with his jacket. When he got back to camp he had to borrow a jacket as there was no tailor to make one.

Returning on the Detroit steamer to Buffalo, they ran into a storm so violent it carried off one of the paddle wheels with such a frightening roar and rending of wood and metal, causing almost complete chaos in the engine room and some very uncomfortable moments on deck.

Even a dedicated plant hunter such as Douglas could not miss a visit to the famous Niagara Falls. He was, of course, very impressed but seemed to find a particularly nice red cedar growing out of the rocks a little more interesting. He also picked a viola.

From Niagara he took another long journey to Philadelphia to visit the home of his eminent predecessor, John Bartram. He saw in his garden a Cypress, 90ft high and 23ft round which John Bartram had planted himself. Douglas then took the coach for South Amley in New Jersey. The coach broke down and took two hours to repair, and to make up for lost time the drivers raced their horses to cover 29 miles in 3 hours.

By December 12 he was on his way home with his collection and arrived in London on January 10 1824. He brought a selection of fruit trees, oaks and other plants, including penstemons. The Society were overjoyed with his finds which were well beyond their expectations.

There was, however, no time to sit and rest. The Horticultural Society were soon sending him back to America, this time under the patronage of the Hudson Bay Company. He set sail from Gravesend on board the William and Ann, a Hudson Bay brig destined for the entrance to the Columbia River. He was fortunate in making friends with a fellow traveller, John Scouler M.D., who had taken the post of surgeon to the ship so that he might follow his first love, Botany and Natural History.

It seemed inevitable that something would go wrong, and it did. Only two days out they hit the Nare shifting sands, and the ship shuddered and shook and 14" of angry salt water filled the hold. Fortunately the pumps held out and they were soon able to sail on. Near Cape Verde Islands it was 86 degrees in his cabin but had only the thermometer to watch and his books to read. They crossed the Equator on September 9 and Neptune called as usual with all that entails. This was more enjoyable than when, a few days later, the sea broke over the whole ship and no one on board, including Douglas, got any rest. The storm passed and was almost forgotten when they sighted the wonderful Sugar Loaf mountain and glimpsed their first view of Rio Harbour on September 28.

Douglas was soon wandering around the foothills accompanied by his new found friend, Scouler, and were unable to believe their eyes on seeing the vast array of plants before them. The wonderful orchids, begonias and gesnerias were breath-taking. He spent the next twelve days collecting specimens of bulbs etc. One gesneria he called 'Sabina' after his old master in London. All these he packed there and then and had them transported back to England, remembering to keep them dry.

Cape Horn, graveyard of many a ship, now loomed ahead. Douglas felt fear, as did everyone else on board, and they were not disappointed. The ship heaved and rolled for about ten days with waves frequently breaking over the ship's sides and there was no rest or sleep of course, and everyone ended up feeling very wet, tired and suffering from fatigue, after their encounters with the freezing cold, howling winds and driving icy winds.

On December 14 they sighted the island of Mas-A-Fuera, a bleak dark bare rock with nowhere to land and therefore decided to carry on to the island of Juan Fernandez.

After rounding the Horn they called in at Juan Fernandez for water and fresh supplies and whilst there Douglas took the opportunity to collect another 80 plants - ferns, tree ferns, escallonias, berberis, lobelia etc.

Christmas came and went and was best remembered for dining on fresh goat meat. On January 9 1825 they were all very pleased indeed to be able once again to stretch their legs at Chatham Island, a classic island which could be called the Madeira of the South Seas. It was very mountainous and volcanic, with burnt red volcanic soil and dark lush green vegetation. This was a very recently discovered island in the Pacific and it was found to be very rich in birds and plants. The birds were so tame that they settled on his hands and the barrel of his gun.

He collected about 135 plant specimens but lost all except for a few seeds in the bad weather that followed.

On February 16 they hit a rain squall so heavy they were able to collect enough water to provide plenty for drinking and even for a bath of sorts. At times the weather seemed to be even worse than that encountered around Cape Horn. By April 2, the "William and Ann" was blown some 170 miles off course out into the Pacific and it was not until April 17 that they were able to enter the mouth of the Columbia River to reach Cape Disappointment and anchor at Bakers Bay. Thus a voyage of eight months and fourteen days was almost at an end.

They sailed up river to the Hudson Bay Company depot at Fort George, but waited until morning before disembarking. It was wonderful to sleep without the ever-present motion and noise of the ship, and everyone slept well. Little did Douglas know that from then on there would be little peace.

Setting foot on land the next morning his eyes were met with a wondrous sight, flowers and plants covered every rock and crevice for miles, forests of great pines and under their dense and luxuriant cover, grew more flowers. He explored further around Fort George and found the forests opened up into lush swamps with even more rare plants and flowers.

It was two days before he saw his first native Red Indian. He had copper and shells hanging from his nose and ears, jet black hair hanging over his shoulders and wore a rough cloak of marmot skin. Douglas watched him and made a mental note that these people were the real guardians of this wonderful wilderness. He noted in his diary "the Indians greeted us with presents of dried salmon, fresh sturgeon and various kinds of dried berry for which we gave them trinkets, bread and molasses".

On April 19 he made the first of a great many trips up river by canoe made of animal skins stretched over a rough wooden frame. On the fast flowing Columbia River, the canoe, manned by six Indians, and full of all his blankets, boxes, drying kits and clothes seemed so overloaded that it was a wonder they did not sink; but the Indians were very experienced canoe men and knew what they were doing.

Sleep was taken in short spells in the bottom of the canoe when the Indians pulled either on to the bank or a sandbank for a short rest. The strong strokes of the Indians took them through beautiful but wild scenery, pine forests, mountains, high cliffs, low swamp plains and rock strewn

The Great Falls by the Multnomah River and Grand Rapids

rapids. Douglas began to realise the great botanical treasures that were there just for the taking.

When they reached Fort Vancouver, ninety miles from the sea, around midnight, he was given a tent which was to be his home for a while at this far outpost of the Company. There was a heavily built wooden stockade around the Fort with a look-out post at each corner indicating that the territory could change from friendly to distinctly hostile. In the centre of the stockade was a large wooden building and it was here that trappers, both Indian and white, came to exchange their skins for cash or goods. At first Douglas only made short trips out into the wilderness to familiarise himself with the surrounding countryside as he had already been warned that it could be very dangerous to wander too far away.

The scenery was breathtaking, high wooded hills and valleys, and the mountains, Hood, St.Helens, Vancouver and Jefferson all had beautiful snow covered peaks. Douglas spent most of his time collecting many species of ribes, berberis, acer and pyrola.

By August he was beginning to find he even enjoyed roughing it, and he made many journeys further and further away from the Fort ignoring the dangers. He took a tent and slept when possible in his upturned canoe, but by far his best idea of sleep was under the pines wrapped only in his blanket. He found 140 shrubs and plants around the Fort and another 300 on a visit to Menzies Island, in the middle of the Columbia River.

He knew he had another great and arduous journey to undertake in the near future. So on June 20 he set forth to the Great Falls by the Multnomah River and Grand Rapids. He had been told before leaving that this was a mad river. One moment they were battling through white water hardly able to hold their paddles, falling into deep gullies, some of which were banked on either side by cliffs that seemed to be 800ft or more high, the next into a perfectly calm stretch of water which almost at once fell away again into large whirlpools and eddies. The changes in scenery were vast from gigantic pines to flat waste land, but he found some plants that he was looking for, e.g. clarkia, spiraea, nicotiana, and penstemons. His diet consisted mainly of small fish, biscuits and the occasional wild chicken which his Indian companions were able to catch.

One night Douglas was invited to sleep in a nearby Indian camp, but during the night several tribesmen were killed and others wounded. Another evening about 300 Indians wearing eagle feather head dresses and carrying bows and arrows were dancing themselves into a frenzied war dance. They had bone knives hanging from their belts and in the light of the burning fires they looked very fearsome.

Next morning there were a great many canoes and about 500 warriors were spotted coming down the river but fortunately peace reigned.

Douglas wrote "the principal chief of the village was Cockqua, he was very friendly with me, he built me a small cabin in his own lodge, he was so interested in my safety he sat and watched me all night in case a war party came".

Douglas's Indians advised him to return to the comparative safety of Fort Vancouver and he quickly made his departure, arriving back at the Fort on August 5 with the majority of his plant and seed finds intact.

He waited until August 18, drying the plants he had collected, and making short journeys in search of seeds and other plants, even though greatly hampered by heavy rain. On the 19th he left the Fort and journeyed up the Multnomah River, a fine river with very fertile banks. On the way he killed a white tailed deer and some black tailed deer.

Two days journey took him to the Calapooie Indian nation, a very peaceful and well-disposed people. He found in the Indians' tobacco pouches, some seeds of a remarkably large pine which they were chewing like nuts. He learnt from them that this pine grew in the forests far to the South. A few days later Douglas returned to Fort Vancouver laden with very many more of his treasured plants and seeds.

On the odd occasions when Douglas had a quiet moment he would often reflect on the life and the career he had chosen. He thought of the dangers, the hunger and fatigue, he had endured on his journeys but to him there were great compensations such as exploring unknown territory, and he loved the challenge of crossing rapids and rivers and the excitement of finding new varieties of plants and collecting seeds. Whilst exploring the

Multnomah River he first came across the mighty monarchs of the forest, i.e. tall and majestic pines. Often he could not collect the perfect seed cones he needed as the trees towered some 300 feet above him. They were very often covered in snow, and rainbows danced between them in the sunlight. That evening he sat by his fire cooking a 30lb salmon which he had bought from an Indian friend for a few pence.

The same fish would have cost a great deal more in England, and of course, how much better it tasted cooked under the shadow of the mighty pines by the river on an open fire, surrounded by his faithful Indians, whose appearance would have looked so fearsome to the European eye, Douglas felt happy and relaxed and went to sleep on a bed of pine branches.

After sleeping too well one night he awoke in the morning horrified to find the bottom had burnt out of his kettle, and that a life saving cup of tea was in jeopardy. Ever resourceful, he unscrewed the lid from his tinder box and used this as a temporary kettle.

He had by now become well acquainted with the Indians whose territory he crossed and travelled in constantly. Many had never seen a white man, and they were not too keen on him travelling across their hunting grounds, and he had to treat them with great respect. They were very inquisitive, sometimes treacherous, and would murder when they knew they could get away with it. The more friendly Indians had a name for him, OLLA-PISKA, in Chinook this means Fire. The Indians thought he could drink boiling water, but which was in fact effervescent salts, and to them his mug of tea was also boiling water.

On his return visit to Cockqua, the principal chief of the Chencok and Chochall tribes, was extremely proud to welcome all Chiefs from King George - a name he had learned from either one of the Vancouver expeditions, or from the crews of other English ships. Cockqua greeted Douglas with the word Clanchouie, their word for friendship, and warmly shook his hand.

The tribe built a large fire which they sat around enjoying a drink of water and tucking into a delicious sturgeon which was about 10 foot in length. After the meal Douglas spent a peaceful night in a tent kindly supplied by the Chief in his honour.

As was the custom, one of the Indians hoping to impress their guest, showed his prowess by shooting an arrow through a 6" grass hoop thrown in the air. No mean feat, and the Chief boasted that no Chief of King George could better it. Douglas primed his gun, and spotting an eagle about 50 yds away perched in a tree, threw a stone and shot the bird dead whilst it was on the wing. The Indians put their hands over their mouths in astonishment and disbelief, and perhaps, tinged with a little fear.

Cladsap, the Indian who shot the arrow still seemed unconvinced and was a little angry at being outdone by their guest. Douglas, therefore, handed him his hat and indicated that he threw it high in the air, and taking aim blew the hat into many pieces. There were now no doubts that Douglas was a great Chief and he was presented with rough baskets and drinking cups plus the Chief's hat to replace his own which was destroyed. The Chief seemed proud of the fact that his hat had been made by one of his relatives, a young girl of twelve, and she also promised Douglas that she would make some hats for him, as worn by his Chief - King George.

After a few more days spent collecting plants Douglas left but before leaving presented Cockqua with gifts of tobacco, knives, nails and flints, but he had difficulty in convincing the Chief that his gun was not for sale and it was obvious that the chief was very disappointed.

Waving his friends good-bye he set forth up river by canoe to Vancouver, a journey which took him two and a half days due to his many stops collecting more plants.

Many weeks later when Douglas next saw his Indian friend, Cockqua true to his promise presented him with three hats made in the English style by the little twelve year old Indian girl. This pleased Douglas very much and after exchanging words of friendship he presented the Chief with some blankets and gave some needles, beads, rings and pins to the little girl for her kindness in making the hats. Cockqua also made Douglas very happy when he handed over a large packet containing seeds of a type of which he had been searching for a long time.

On another of his plant hunting trips in August the temperature rose to 97 degrees in the shade. He suffered much from this heat and the reflection from the sun on the sand. By the end of the day his feet were so bad they had developed into one big blister. His consolation was in the plants he found, some every day, common examples of today's border plants including penstemon, phlox, hypericum, arabis, and veronica. On or about August 18 he dried and parcelled his plants and seeds and set sail with his Indian friends and cargo down the rapids of the Multnomah River, often carrying canoe and goods strapped to their heads, as there was no safe beach to walk on. It was only a short trip for Douglas, as by September 5 he was back at home base.

After a short rest he set off again, this time on a three day trek back to the mountains. The way was rough, over dead wood, rocks and rivers. He took with him 3 ounces of tea, one pound of sugar and four small biscuits. The route was so difficult, and the night closed in before he reached the summit. The night passed well and comfortable, having dined on an eagle, tea made in an open kettle and drinking from a dish made from bark, and with a good fire he slept well. Next day he filled the Indian pouches with seeds from three new pines he found. The next evening the Indians did not realise this and put his precious seeds on the fire.

On his arrival back at Fort Vancouver, exciting news greeted Douglas - a ship from England was in the Columbia Estuary. He was so excited he hurriedly packed all his seeds, specimens and some Indian dresses, in all sixteen bundles and cases.

In fact he was working so hard at it that he snagged his knee on a rusty nail sticking out of a packing case. So bad was it that he was laid up for three weeks with a badly swollen knee joint and an abscess. He sent a message to the ship's captain to make sure all the cases were kept well above the water line of the ship, but with a sufficient amount of circulating air.

Douglas was very disappointed not to be able to see his best fried, John

Scouler, whom he was told was on board. Determined as he was, he persuaded four Indians to take him at top speed to reach the ship some eighty miles to the sea. They hoped to do it in just over two days and nights, but unfortunately they struck a hidden stump in the river which split the canoe. They had to stop and gum and repair it but again sped off through the night only to find on arrival the ship had sailed one hour before.

On the return journey they encountered a huge storm, their canoe overturned loosing all their food etc. They dragged the canoe as best they could, and when they reached Cape Disappointment they had to drag, pull and carry the canoe for over four miles, over rocks and stumps. They camped for one night at the Cape. Douglas's knee was by now giving him great pain and discomfort after all the exertion. Having not been able to find food they decided to travel on to Cape Foulweather, it was a journey of some forty miles along the coast and there they met with a hurricane, sleet and hail. As darkness fell they decided to make camp whilst the hurricane continued to pound them.

Douglas had to move camp when the sea rose too high for comfort. They had to stay there for three days, clothes soaking wet, very little protection except for a few pine branches, wet blankets and very little fire due to the high winds and rains and no food. Before daylight on the third day they were ready to leave Cape Foulweather. A place, he said later, totally deserved its name. They then walked sixteen miles to Whitbys Harbour, hoping to find fish but when they arrived there were no fish. All they could find to eat were berries and fruit, but Douglas was able to build a shelter out of pine branches and light a large fire, enabling them to dry their clothes and blankets. His knee was, by now so painful that he was forced to spend a whole day resting it. He felt better for his rest and the warm fire and by evening felt strong enough to go out shooting and bagged some ducks. After cooking them he found he had no appetite for eating them. The large fire attracted the attention of some friends who sent a canoe across the river for them and Douglas was very grateful to them for enabling him to rest in their camp for a few days and eat the food they had to spare.

On November 7, he started up the Cheecheeler River in another canoe with an Indian guide. They travelled sixty miles up river in a deluge of rain, which rather cooled his botanical ardour for a while. He disembarked, paid off his guide with the canoe, and hired another guide with pack horses to carry his baggage to the Cowlitz River, a journey of about forty miles. This took two very hard days walking through almost impenetrable forest, and because of the heavy rain, rivulets were running through the paths making everything soaking wet. As if this was not enough they had to strip off and wade through deep water holding their clothes and the precious bundles of seeds aloft to keep them as dry as possible; losing quite a lot. They were beginning to feel very hungry for as usual food was in short supply.

A Chinook Indian Chief, Com-comly gave them a canoe and twelve Indians to ferry them across the river, together with some dried salmon, roots, berries and a goose to help them reach their base, Fort Vancouver, in safety. Douglas rigged up his coat as a sail, and they made good headway on the fast flowing Columbia River, arriving very bedraggled after an absence of a month.

Christmas came and went, but Douglas being a true Scot celebrated the New Year 1826 as best he could, however his knee was still hurting so he could only watch the festivities and had to decline when the others went for a horse ride through the snow. All botany had ceased for the time being.

Douglas was now in his 27 year and was feeling very low for such a young man.

As spring began to arrive the Horticultural Society wanted him to come home. This he felt he could not do as he so enjoyed the splendour of the snow capped mountain, banked with such magnificent pines and carpeted with such an abundance of plants and flowers. So many birds could be seen flying around that they clouded out the sun at times. No way could he leave this wondrous place un-trodden by white man. In this situation monetary rewards meant nothing to Douglas - he was quite prepared to stay another year without pay, or at least just enough to keep himself clothed.

Feeling better for his rest he packed up all his seeds - by now well over a hundred pounds in weight - plus plants and specimens and sent then on their way to England.

His next aim was to reach the Rocky Mountains, some eight hundred miles away. So on March 20 1826, he left Fort Vancouver, and took with him two boats and about a dozen men. His friends waved them off, but as they travelled down river they knew there were hostile Indians watching them from behind the trees and bushes all the way. Not much sleep was had as at all times someone had to keep watch with a cocked gun. Time passed without too much anguish and he was able to sit and write to Doctor Hooker, telling him he was very short of clothing, possessing only two shirts, a blanket, a coat, two pairs of breeches and a cloak, but waxed rapturously over the sugar pines he had found. They rose to 250 feet and had a circumference of over 50 feet. Their cones were 18" long.

They reached the falls skirting the Rocky mountains on March 24 and from here to Walla Walla (the first inland post) the country was very rocky, hilly and lacking in trees, the soil sandy and barren, the banks of the river were also very rocky. He walked along the banks when possible and found a beautiful new lily, and a new species of wulfenia. They also saw a few species of deer, bears, wolves, foxes and badgers.

The party pushed further and further north and Douglas began to feel the cold once more and at times the snow was 5 feet deep. They reached the junction of Spokane River on April 11 where he packed up more plants, seeds and all his notes and sent them on their way to England via the Hudson Bay Company.

On April 22 they arrived at Fort Colville near Kettle Falls and by May 9 they were ready to set off northwards again taking with them three horses, dried buffalo meat, tea and sugar. One horse carried the provisions, the other blankets, papers, specimen bags, containers etc. He managed to find two willing guides, but another hazardous journey was in prospect. The weather was wet and cold, with rapids and waterfalls to be crossed and definitely no place for horses. Most of the time they were waist deep in water holding the luggage above their heads. After being in water of 40 degrees they crawled to the bank and made a huge fire to dry out as best they could.

Next morning on May 11, they started out long before dawn for Spokane, and by 7 o'clock they had reached the summit of the hills. Douglas found his flintlock had been damaged, this he could not do without. Fortunately, a M. Jacques Finlay, the only person who could repair it within a radius of 800 miles lived in the camp and although he could not speak a word of English, he was very satisfied to receive payment of a pound of tobacco. Douglas spent a few days here and returned to Kettle Falls on Sunday, May 14.

He set off to find more plants and seeds and found another un-named pine, some good plants and more penstemons. One of these he called Scouleri, after his friend. By this time the temperature had reached 86 degrees. It was a good idea to find time to sleep before setting off again down the rapids, which were running fast with the melting mountain snow. He slept for about four hours before setting off on the next part of his journey. The current was so fast they travelled the Thomson Rapids, nearly one hundred miles in eight hours. Stopping on route he was given a large amount of tobacco by the local Indians, and this was gratefully received as it would come in very handy for bargaining for food, canoes and guides.

When at last he returned to Fort Vancouver he found two letters from England, which made him very excited and repeatedly read them until late into the night.

On June 16 Douglas set off for the Blue Mountains in Oregon, a journey of some one hundred and fifty miles southwards this time. They walked about forty miles a day and slept as best they could at night, being plagued by either rats or ants both of enormous size. They managed to reach the mountain summit and found the weather at 9000 feet damp and dismal with thunder and lightening, so they returned down to where they had made camp as quickly as the soft snow would allow. The guides refused to go any further so there was no alternative but to return to base camp. Douglas was now suffering with pain in his eyes, firstly from sand and now from snow blindness. He did, however, find a beautiful peony and a lupin that he had not seen anywhere else.

At the end of July he set out again for Spokane, this time with Canadian guides who spoke very little English and a few horses. They then travelled off to Kettle Falls arriving on August 5. Unfortunately he lost most of his precious collection when some of the horses fell into the river.

In September he heard that there was a ship from England in Columbia. At Kettle Falls he had a great many seeds, plants and specimens, nearly 200 in all, so he decided to get them to the ship as quickly as possible, a distance of some 200 miles. The Indians agreed to allow him to pass from tribe to tribe overland to the sea. At the end of August he arrived, having lost only a few specimens, but these were replaced as he had found a few new ones on the way.

Douglas stayed near the junction of the Lewis and Clarms River with Columbia until July 8, but was getting tired of this barren part of the country with scarcely any food and no plants of any interest. Fishing was impossible because the water was too high to throw a line or cast a net and horse meat became the only food available. Travelling down the river to the Great Falls, the party had the good fortune to meet a small fleet of boats on their way to the interior carrying letters from England for Douglas. He returned to Walla Walla on July 15.

In September, he decided to make another trip to Oregon. This meant more hostile Indian country and all that this entailed. The Indians, some well over 6ft tall, wearing large eagle feathers, war paint and carrying bows and arrows, presented a very frightening picture. Perhaps they too thought that Douglas, carrying his rifle and wearing homemade deerskin trousers, shirt, hat and shoes also looked formidable. Whilst out plant-hunting one day his horse slipped and fell and Douglas hurt his leg very badly. He could only walk using a branch and his musket as crutches aided by a young Indian.

By now it was October again, most of the time he was wet, cold and hungry, in pain and existing on one meal a day. One night a violent thunderstorm occurred, pines fell all around amidst great flashes of lightening, and even the horses continually neighed in terror. However, by dawn the skies had cleared and he was able to continue his journey through the forest and found to his joy one of the mightiest pine trees had fallen during the storm enabling him to collect some of its cones which, due to the trees great height had previously eluded him.

Douglas had to be on his guard at all times, for even as he worked he could see the fires of the Indians. If they came out of the forest with their bows drawn and their knives hanging on their wrists, he knew that meant only one thing - beat a hasty retreat. One day he offered them some horse meat but they were not impressed, wanting only dog meat.

November found him back at Fort Vancouver. By Christmas he was a very sick, frail man, injuries, the wet and cold, lack of food and sleep had all taken their toll. From Christmas until February 1827 he spent the time recuperating and getting back some of his strength whilst waiting for the snows to melt. Douglas wanted to make one last long journey from coast to coast, travelling from the Pacific Ocean to the Atlantic Ocean, then, all being well, to go home. By 1825 he had already trekked over 2000 miles on mostly un-trodden tracks. By 1826 he had journeyed 4000 miles from Vancouver to Kettle Falls exploring many side tracks in search of any plants that might be of interest risking his life almost daily in his pursuit.

On March 20 1827 he set out on his long journey by foot, horseback and canoe, having been fitted out and clothed by the Hudson Bay Company. The first twenty-five days he travelled on foot, through deep fir woods, across sandy plains, passing rivers and lakes collecting botany specimens. At times he had to take to the river but avoided travelling this way as much as possible.

In the distance, the great divide-the Rocky Mountains stood between Douglas and his destination Jasper House.

Eventually he reached Fort Colville, and after resting set off on April 18 on the next stage of his journey to cross the great divide - the Rocky Mountains. He was making for Jasper House in the Rocky Mountains a distant of 350 miles. As he set out snow was beginning to fall. This time he was forced to travel some distance by canoe encountering rapids and some very strong currents and was eventually very glad to be back on land even though it meant wearing snow shoes. The snow was 4 feet deep in places with the added danger of river ice being so thin that he could feel it cracking under his weight. He was not used to walking in snow shoes and kept falling over. Douglas had to juggle to keep his precious specimens dry. At times he was so cold and wet his clothes froze to his back. After lighting a large fire each evening to dry his clothes and blankets, he slept on fir branches with damp blankets. Despite all the hazards he managed to reach Jasper House on May 4.

Mr McDonald, a friend of Douglas accompanied him as a guide on one of his hunting expeditions for meat. During the hunt he was badly mauled by a wild bull, and received injuries to his left leg, broken ribs, a broken left wrist and severe bruising. Fortunately McDonald was almost unconscious with his very painful injuries and the bull lost interest in the lifeless body. As all this happened during the hours of darkness the rescue of his friend was made more difficult, especially as the bull hovered in close proximity. However, Douglas fired a few shots and the animal reluctantly ambled away. Douglas then bound McDonald's wounds as best he could and as soon as possible they managed to stagger to Carlton House to seek proper medical attention.

After a very short rest they set off again for Fort Edmonton via the Saskatchewan River. At one place the river was so deep and fast flowing they had to rope one of the team, who went across first and the others then followed safely but with difficulty. After a walk of 50 miles with nothing to eat they arrived tired and hungry at Fort Edmonton and dined that evening on moose steaks.

Still on the Saskatchewan River they now made for Lake Winnipeg. Douglas was still, of course, collecting seeds and specimens. One beautiful evergreen he found had its branches festooned with catkins well over a foot long and this he named after the Secretary of the Hudsons Bay Company - Hudson Garry, who had been so kind to him and looked after him so well.

On September 15 1827 Douglas left Hudson Bay for England. His patrons, Sabine, Hooker and the Horticultural Society were overwhelmed with his success, beyond their wildest dreams.

By now he was so tired and weak that most of the journey home was spent resting in his cabin. He arrived at Portsmouth on October 11 1827 and his fame had certainly gone before him. There were so many people to greet him and an even larger crowd greeted his arrival in London.

For his outstanding contributions to botany he was made a Fellow of the Society. A great honour for as he put it - "just a Scottish gardener".

Douglas spent his time now helping the Horticultural Society to arrange his plants and specimens and planting seeds, but it was, of course, too much to expect Douglas to sit back and rest on his laurels. Soon they were discussing another trip, this time to map and survey for the Colonial Office. They supplied him with all the instruments as well as giving him a salary. So once again he set off on a long voyage around Cape Horn with all the dangers this entailed. He reached his old base, Fort Vancouver, on June 3 1830.

The rest had done him the world of good and he felt a new man. He also had a little terrier as a friend. His new found strength saw him on his travels again; in almost every direction and with renewed vigour finding many new pines, specimens and seeds. In October 1830 he despatched four large chests containing his finds to London.

While he was away some unscrupulous fur traders had upset some of the Indian tribes which created a lot of bad blood between them. Some had turned hostile and some fought amongst themselves due mostly to them being given strong liquor. This made life very dangerous for Douglas travelling with only his Indian guide and the little terrier. He now decided life was getting a bit too dangerous and left for California. He landed in San Francisco in 1831 and from there he travelled to Monteray where he enlisted the help of local Monks and their knowledge of the countryside.

Douglas found California an "Aladdins Cave" of finds as it was here he first saw the mighty redwood trees. He was the first person to describe their magnitude and splendor and their great age in detail. Douglas also found another four hundred species of plants, flowers and shrubs.

It was in these forests he found the mighty pine that carries his name, the Douglas Fir.

In December 1833 Douglas again visited Hawaii, which was also known at the time as The Sandwhich Islands, arriving in Woahu on December 27. Whilst still on board ship he was visited by an American missionary named Mr Spalding who invited him that day to visit his mission situated on a hillside approximately 500 feet above sea level. In the evening he thanked his host, saying how much he admired his work before returning to sleep on board ship. Unfortunately he records that he managed very little sleep due to the agonising pains of rheumatism caused by the endless hours spent over the past in wet clothes. On January 7 1834 - never one to succumb to pain - Douglas started his long awaited exploration of Hawaii, deciding to climb the two extinct volcanos of Mauna Kea and Mauna Loa.

He decided to climb Mauna Kea first and was enthralled by the ferns, the creeping vines and the lush vegetation, and above all, the beautiful palm trees. He was in his element collecting many species of plants, and revelled in the hot sun and the feel of the warm sea breezes on his face, after enduring cold and snow for so long. However, a sudden heavy rain shower surprised him and he was forced to seek shelter in an abandoned saw mill where he ate his lunch.

Ignoring the heavy rain Douglas decided to continue his climb but the paths were more treacherous and very narrow in places. He spent the night in a small hut but was unable to find any dry wood to light a fire and he spent a miserable night in his wet clothes.

The following day was fine but the air was colder. Climbing several thousand feet higher he came upon two wild cattle hunters, a Mr Miles and Mr Castle. Both men were curing the fresh meat of wild cattle which abounded on the mountain sides. Douglas was offered rest and to warm himself by the large fire, which he gladly accepted. Next day his two acquaintances invited him to go shooting the wild cattle, but they spent most of their time smoking their pipes and sitting down talking. This did not please Douglas and he wandered off but did not fail to notice the huge herds of wild cattle in the area. These cattle were all descendants of the stock left by Captain Vancouver for which the islanders were very grateful.

Continuing his exploration of the mountain peak and collecting what specimens he could find of the many plants. He observed several caves in the area and wandered over to inspect them. He found that some were used by the natives as living quarters and others were used to house their stocks of pigs and goats.

In the enriched soil plants grew in profusion and some of the natives had tilled small plots of land in which they grew tobacco, Indian corn, melons and other fruits.

On July 12 1834, he climbed the north side of Mauna Loa carrying a stout stick accompanied by his constant companion, the little terrier, and his friend Ned who was acting as guide. Wild cattle still abounded on the mountain slopes and the paths seemed even more dangerous and narrower than those on Mauna Kea. The recent heavy rains had also turned the paths to thick mud. The guide accompanied Douglas for about a mile up the mountain but showed concern over the many wild cattle he had to skin on his return. Douglas not anticipating any real danger allowed him to return to his work. The guide's parting words to Douglas warned him to be especially careful of the dangerous paths and the perilous wild bull traps.

Perhaps due to his infatuation with collecting new plant species Douglas failed to notice the low clouds sweeping in and the mist thickening. All dangers being ignored his feet suddenly shot from under him and he was sliding out of control and into one of the bull traps with their sheer sides.

Unfortunately the trap had already claimed a victim, a young bull which was by no means dead. The animal presumably panicked and being wild started a frenzied attack on Douglas as he lay helpless. The steepness of the trap walls and in such a confined space Douglas stood no chance as the terrified animal continued to trample him. Many hours later some natives, checking the traps noticed a leg covered in dirt and blood and such was the condition of the rest of the body that they thought it was one of the natives. They ran down the mountainside to get help from his friend Ned who brought his gun and shot the animal.

They rescued the body from the pit, carried it wrapped in an animal skin gently back to Ned's house. Nearby they found Douglas's little terrier, crouched down and still guarding a bundle containing his last botanical finds.

At the mission whilst they were carefully washing the body, unrecognisable from its trampling by the wild bull, they discovered that it was a white man, who they realised was Douglas.

The little terrier lived out his life on Hawaii well cared for by Douglas's friend, Ned.

H.M.S. Challenger, under the command of Captain Seymour conveyed his body to his funeral in Honolulu where members from the mission and his friends paid their last respects. A stone memorial was later erected in his memory.

No other collector reaped such a vast harvest of plants in America. You only have to walk through any of our great gardens or stately homes to see the living memorial to Douglas in the magnificent pines, firs and spruces as well as the many flowers - a tribute in themselves to one of the greatest plant hunters of all times, second only to George Don.

David Douglas, aged 34, was buried in Honolulu on August 14 1834. The sad task of writing to his family was left to the Govenor of the Sandwich Isalnds.(Hawaii)

When you look at the flowers in your own garden, I hope you will see them now in a different light. Common flowers such as potentilla, clarkia, californian poppy, antirrhinum, godetia, lupin and spirea to name but a few; and last but by no means least penstemons.

If David Douglas had lived to write his life history it would, no doubt have turned out to be one of the most fantastic adventure stories of all time.

The following penstemons were found mostly in N W America and California. Some can still be found today, but the majority have been hybridised into the large garden penstemons we know today e.g.

P acminatus	P grandiflorus
P albidus	P heterophyllus
P attenuatus	P linear if ol ia
P breviflorus	P menziesii var Douglasii
P centranthifolius	P ovatus
P coeruleus	P phacelia tanacentifolia
P confertus	P pruinosus
P crassifolius	P richardsonii
P deustus	P scouleri
P diffusus	P serrulatus
P digitalifolius	P speciosus
P frutescens	P staticifolius
P glaber	P triphyllus
P glandulosus	P venustus
P gracilis	

The American Penstemon

As previously mentioned Penstemons are found growing in the two extremes of climate, scorching hot deserts and freezing wind swept mountain sides with only the warmth of deep snow to keep them alive. Humming birds appear to be very partial to the nectar of Penstemons and in consequence aid their pollinisation. Strangely they seem to have a preference for the hot colours i.e. reds and pinks whereas the wasps and bees, especially the carpenter bee are not so fussy and will seek their nectar from any coloured flower but have a slight preference for the colder colours i.e. blues and purples. The P.Scarlet Bugler *(centranthifolius)* is a typical choice of the humming bird with its small projecting lobes although it is beardless and without guidelines to the nectar. Apart from the nectar, bees find the flowers of Penstemons an ideal place for rest and shelter from the rain, and certain wasps use the plants to build a small nest and deposit an egg. To most animals the penstemon tastes very bitter and they are rarely grazed, even the humble slug seems to give them a wide berth.

A short list of the more popular Penstemons found in America today. For the readers interest I have listed what I think are the more well known Penstemons originating in their native country.

centranthifolius

P. ambiguus
P. albious
P. alpinus
P. angustiflosius
P. attenuatus
P. aridus
P. azureus
P. alluviorum
P. barbatus-yellow
P. barbatus-red
P. barbatus-elfin pink
P. barrettiae
P. barnebyi
P. campanulatus
P. calycosus
P. centranthifolius
P. cardwelli
P. coroifolia
P. caroinalis
P. caespitosus
P. confertus
P. comarrhenus.
P. cobeae
P. clutei
P. crandallii
P. concinnus
P. clevelandii
P. cyaneus
P. cyananthus
P. davidsonii
P. digitalis
  (Huskers Red)
P. eatonii
P. eximeus
P. florious
P. fruticosus
P. gaironerii
P. gracilis

P. grandiflorus
P. grinnelli
P. glaber
P. hirsutus
P. heterophyllus
P. hartwegi
P. hartwegi Albus
P. haydenii
P. humilis (mesa)
P. hallii
P. harbourii
P. isophyllus
P. jamesii
P. janishiae
P. jonessi
P. keckiella (White)
P. kuntheii
P. laricifolius
P. leonardii
P. laevis
P. laxiflorus
P. linarioides
P. lyallii (Purple)
P. laetus (roezllii)
P. laevigatus (White)
P. montanus
P. newberryii
P. neotericus
P. nitidus
P. oklahomensis
P. ovatus
P. ophianthus
P. parvulus
P. petiolatus
P. pruinosus
P. procerus
P. palmeri
P. pallious
P. praeteritus

P. payettensus
P. pinifolius
  (Merses Yellow)
P. prairie fire
P. purpussii
P. Rose elf
P. rostriflorus
P. rubicundus
P. rubicola
P. richardsonii
P. ryobergii
P. serrulatus
P. secundiflorus
P. sepalulus
P. strictus
P. smallii
P. schooleys (Yellow)
P. scoulerii
P. scoulerii albus
P. spectabilis
P. speciosus
P. Stapleford Gem
P. scharf hybrids
P. tenuiflorus
P. tubaeflorus
P. tenuis
P. teucriodes
P. thompsonii
P. triaphyllus
P. vespoides
P. venustus
P. virens
P. virgatus
P. wizlizenii
P. whippleanus
P. weelerii
P. wilcoxii
P. watsonii

Penstemons as Listed by George Don in 1831

NAME	FOUND BY	WHERE FOUND
P. acuminatum	Douglas	N.W.America - sandy plains on the Columbia River
P. albidum	Nuttal	Missouri plains and river plate to the mountains
P. atropurpurum	Don	Mexico
P. attenuatum	Douglas	N.W.America - mountains of lewis and Clark's River
P. barbatum	Nuttal	Mexico
P. caeruleum	Nuttal	Missouri plains near Fort Mandan
P. campanulatus	Willd	Mexico near Santa Rosa de la Sierra and Los Joares
P. centianoides	Don	Mexico
P. centranthifolium	Benth	California
P. christatum	Nuttal	Teeton River and The Missouri to the mountains
P. cobaea	Nuttal	N. American prairies of Red River and Texas
P. confertum	Douglas	N.W.America mountainous pine forests, Salmon River and Kettle Falls on Columbia River
P. cordifolium	Douglas	California
P. deustum	Douglas	N.W.America on scorched rocky plains in the interior
P. diffusum	Douglas	N.W.America - districts around mouth of Columbia River
P. dissectum	Ell	Georhia and Louisville
P. digitalis	Nuttal	Arkansas wet woods and prairies
P. gentianoides	Don	Mexico on Mount Toluco
P. glabrum	Pursh	N. America near Shian River and towards the Columbia River
P. glaucum	Graham	Arctic and America
P. glandulosum	Douglas	N.America banks of Kooskooskee River
P. graclie	Nuttal	N.America from Arikarees to Fort Mandam

NAME	FOUND BY	WHERE FOUND
P. grandiflorum	Nuttal	Missouri Plains and prairies
P. heterophyllum	Douglas	California
P. hirsutum	Willd	Virginia
P. humboldtii		Mexico between Puerto deVarientos and Santa Rosa
P. kunthii	Don	Mexico near Moran and Omitla
P. laevigatum	Ait	N. America
P. micranthum	Nuttal	N.America Rocky Mountains near source of Columbia River
P. ovatum	Douglas	N.W.America high mountains of Grand Rapis Columbia
P. procerum	Douglas	N.W.America and Rocky Mountains
P. pubescens	Ait	N.America and southern states of Carolina and Georgia
P. pulchellum	Lindl	Mexico between Toluca and Tianquillo and Cuba near Havana
P. pumilum	Nuttal	Source of Columbia river and borders of Little Goddin River
P. pruinosum	Douglas	N.W.America near Priests Rapid on Columbia River
P. richardsonii	Douglas	N.W.America dry rocks in vicinity of Columbia River
P. roseum	Don	Mexico
P. scouleri	Douglas	N.W.America, Kettle Falls of Columbia River
P. speciosum	Douglas	N.W.America on banks of Spokan River
P. staticifolium	Lindl	California
P. triphyllum	Douglas	Northern California, N.W. America, Blue Mountains and Columbia River
P. tubiflorum	Nuttal	Arkansas in wettish prairies from Fort Smith to Red River
P. venustum	Douglas	N.W.America in dried up river beds among mountains

When the first Penstemons were introduced and were listed by such eminent botanists as George Don in his Dichlamydeons Book of Plants (1832) many of them ended "m" "ium" and when they were tested and genders were classified, many changed to "ius" as in today's "Plant Finder" even though being of the same species e.g. Cordifolium - Cordifoloius.

$\mathcal{F}$orbes $\mathcal{C}$atalogue of $\mathcal{P}$enstemons
for 1897

NEW FOR 1897

Atlantis - purple scarlet with large white throat, enormous flowers
Colonel Hope - scarlet veined crimson, extra large flowers of finest form
Catulles Mendes - white, edged salmon, very large
Countess of Ravensworth - purplish rose, white throat, finely edged bronzy chocolate,
    splendid spike
Crafty - a beautiful rose, with scarlet throat
Donald McBean - purplish crimson, white throat, heavily maculated, rich chocolate, very
    large & striking
Dietz Monnin - violet purple, large white throat, pencilled crimson, extra
Dr Mair - rosy purple, white throat, heavily maculated dark crimson, grand spike, extra
    fine
Emile Montegut - scarlet with violet and white, very large open throat, one of the
    grandest varieties ever produced
Forain - clear scarlet, large white throat, veined, large flower and find spike
Froelich - purplish crimson, very large flower, grand spike
General Thomas - rosy cerise, with enormous white throat very large and of perfect form
Henriot - crimson, very large, superb variety
James Robertson - pure white, tinted rose at edges, a fine spike of well formed flowers
Jeanne Mairet - sulphur white, large well-formed flowers, long pyramidal spike
Legende - salmon white, large flowers grand spike
Leonnec - rosy scarlet, white throat blotched crimson
Loredan Larchey - beautiful rosy, white throat maculated, enormous flowers on
    large branching spike
Maitre Antifer - bright rose, throat veined purplish crimson large and very fine
Mrs Daniels - purplish rose with white throat, large open circular flowers, well set on
    tall symmetrical spikes, extra fine
Mrs Hope - violet purple, veined and maculated chocolate, well built spikes of
    finely formed flowers
Mrs Melville - rosy pink, large open white throat, a pleasing and distinct variety
Paul Verlaine - beautiful rose, large open throat bordered rosy scarlet, very
    large and grand
Peter Brock - rosy purple, with a large open white throat, veined crimson,
    magnificent spike
Peter Scott - bright rosy purple, white throat, beautifully veined and bronzy chocolate,
    splendid close set spike
Port Royal - rosy violet, large white throat, of immense size, extra
W H Divers - rosy crimson, veined and blotched crimson, splendid close-set
    pyramidal spike

GENERAL COLLECTION

Alphonse Daudet - purplish crimson, throat pencilled maroon large and fine
Aspasie - rosy scarlet, large white throat, veined, a grand variety
Andrew Sinclair - rosy scarlet, shaded, very fine
Agassiz - beautiful bright red, purple throat, bordered with white, dwarf and fine
Alfred Rambaud (1896) - bright rosy scarlet, large open pure white throat,
    flowers of immense size

Auguste Cain (1896) - very large, scarlet shading to rose white throat, a grand spike
Argrow - bluish purple, white throat, pencilled and blotched dark crimson
Brian Wynne - rosy scarlet white throat veined and blotched crimson, grand spike, extra
Bridesmaid - large well-formed spike of pure white flowers perhaps the purest white in cultivation
Beatrice - bright salmon, white throat, bordered with blue very large
Berlioz - violet purple, white throat, pencilled purple, novel colour, extra
Buccleuch Gem - clear rosy pink, large open white throat, slightly veined purplish crimson, distinct & grand
Bernard Cowan (1896) - rosy crimson throat heavily striped crimson, find spike
Compacta - scarlet, white throat veined chocolate, fine spike
Charles Street - pale lilac, veined and margined reddish crimson
Charles Dickens - scarlet, pure white throat, enormous flowers
Charles Bigot - magenta rose, large white throat, veined with purple crimson, a grand spike
Conspicus - enormous spikes, violet purple, white throat, marked crimson
Cigale - rosy salmon, enormous white throat, grand flowers of perfect form
Countess of Minto (1896) - a beautiful rosy pink, large circular white throat, margined with chocolate, very attractive, extra fine
Ch. Robin - large carmine rose, throat white, veined carmine
Cythere - scarlet, white throat with purple markings, grand flower
Dagnan Bouvert - large white throat, bordered rose, fine spike
Danae - vermilion, white throat, blood veined
De Saussure (1896) - dark purple, with large scarlet throat, very large
Eclipse - crimson, blotched chocolate, large flowers
Emile Augier - scarlet, white throat, veined dark maroon,
Etendard - carmine, white throat, large flower, grand spike
Edward Tyndall - purplish violet, white throat
Emile Deschanel - clear carmine, throat maculated and pencilled blood red, enormous flowers
Emile Paladilhe - crimson, white throat, pencilled crimson
E. Chabier (1896) - a beautiful bright rose, large throat, banded with purple
Falstaff (1896) - a beautiful claret, large expanded throat spotted with maroon
F W Moore - amaranth, white throat, with brown veins, grand
Gaston Bonnier - blue suffused scarlet, white throat, veined with violet
George Davidson - crimson, large, open, white throat, pencilled crimson
G Hahmann - bright crimson, large white throat
Gounod - violet purple, white throat, pencilled and blotched with purple
Gulliver - large white flowers, edged violet, well defined enormous flower of fine form, grand spike
George Groves (1896) - white, suffused with violet
George McLellan(1896) - scarlet, white throat, veined crimson, fine close spike
George Rous - dark purplish violet, with a clear white throat, very large flowers on a compact spike
Gigantea - crimson, shaded purple, heavily pencilled and blotched rich chocolate, very fine
George Reynolds - rich crimson, large open throat, veined bronzy chocolate
George Ulrich - fiery scarlet with white throat
H. Stadtler - rosy violet, white throat surrounded with brown
Henry Lister - purple, white throat, pencilled rich crimson
Herbert Spencer - (1896), rosy scarlet, throat margin maroon, very large and fine
Herodiade (1896) - white with lilac shade, large flowers
Hugh G Oliver - purplish violet white throat, pencilled and margined crimson - enormously large

Juvenal - carmine-scarlet, large maroon circle in the throat
Joanne Chatin - scarlet suffuse purple, white throat, veined purplish crimson
Jean Lorrain (1896) - rosy violet, white throat, veined crimson, large and grand
James Day - scarlet, large, pure white throat, veined and maculated crimson scarlet, a very superior variety
John Foster (1896) - rosy scarlet, with large open white throat
John Fraser (1896) - brilliant rosy scarlet, large open throat, maculated reddish chocolate, close spike
John Young(1896) - rosy scarlet, large open throat, heavily edged fiery chocolate, distinct and grand
John Brown - purplish lilac, open white throat, veined chocolate, close spike, extra grand
John Duncanson - crimson, blotched chocolate, enormous spike
John Laurie - crimson, pure white throat, compact spike
John Ruthven - violet-purple, heavily, large open throat, pencilled chocolate
John Stewart - rosy purple, heavily veined chocolate
John Melville - clear rosy pink, white throat, pencilled and edged chocolate, perfect flower spike
John Harper - clear rosy purple, white throat, veined rosy crimson
John McHattie - rosy violet, flowers of enormous size
Joseph Oliver - violet purple, white throat, heavily blotched crimson
Joseph Bean (1896) - rosy pink, large open white throat, margined chocolate, thickly set on a large spike
Joseph Cockfield - dark crimson, pure white throat
J.M.Troupe - deep purplish crimson, white throat, heavily pencilled crimson and chocolate, very large flowers
Jules Sandeau - bright rosy scarlet, large white throat, margined purple
Lamennals (1896) - carmine-scarlet, throat margined and veined crimson, a variety of great merit
La Masque (1896) - rosy purple, large white throat, edged deep crimson
Le Borda - beautiful violet, throat maroon purple
Le Superbe - bright vermilion, white throat, veined with carmine
Le Niagara - creamy-white, enormous flower spike
Leonidas - rich rose, white throat, beautifully pencilled
Lord Ravensworth - bright rosy purple, suffused bright scarlet, large white throat
Mdlle.A.Singer - violet red, large, veined and striped purple
Madame de Genlis - white, large throat mottled lilac, dwarf
Madame A. Schauffele - pure white, edged with bright crimson
Maggie Porter - rosy scarlet, white throat, veined crimson
More de Venice - clear violet with large pure white throat
Moonshine - white, tinged and edged rosy scarlet
Mrs Bosanquet - crimson, pencilled chocolate, close spike
Mrs Barnes - white, edged lilac, enormous spike
Mrs T.L. Watson - purplish lilac, large open throat
Mrs Burn - rosy scarlet, white throat, pencilled blood crimson
Mrs Coppin - (1896) pale rose, white throat, veined chocolate
Mrs Street - rich rosy scarlet, white throat, pencilled crimson
Mrs Cranston - fine ruby red, white throat large open flowers
Mrs Forbes - orange scarlet, white throat, long close spike of large well opened flowers
Mrs Wood - rosy scarlet, white throat, blotched crimson
Mrs McIndoe - dark crimson, white throat, blotched dark chocolate
Matamore - beautiful scarlet, throat marbled with purple
Mont Blanc - pure white, grand flower
Mousequetaire - large cherry red, pure white throat, blotched carmine, long branching spike

M.Bouley - bright lake, large white throat, veined carmine
Neil McKinnon - rosy scarlet, large open flowers
Onesime Reclus - violet, white throat, veined
Oliver de Serres - pure white, extra large
Oliver Payne - violet, white throat, blotched purple violet
Owen Thomas - bright fiery scarlet, maculated chocolate
Petrarque - creamy white, suffused rose
Perle - clear violet, white throat, striped violet
Pythagore - beautiful violet, white throat, veined with crimson
President Carnot - brilliant scarlet, large open white throat, enormous flower spike
Pretre de Nemi - dark violet, white throat, blotched purple
Quatrelles (1896) - dark rose, white throat, encircled with purple
Renown - rich purple crimson, heavily blotched chocolate
R Schmoll - rosy salmon, veined red, surrounded with carmine
Renommee - clear amaranth, pure white throat
Saintine - rosy purple, white throat encircled with purple
St Mungo - rosy purple, white throat, blotched chocolate
Sesostris - amaranth, purple throat,
Sylphe - white passing to lilac, free flowering
Sandorf - a beautiful claret, large open throat
Serenade - white shaded lilac
Servadoc - grand flowers of a lilac purple, white throat, pencilled and margined with violet
Surcouf - carmine, suffused with lake, white throat, veined chocolate
Scapin (1896) - clear violet with reddish purple blotch in the throat
Tartarin - violet, white throat, bordered purple
Tissandler - carmine, white throat, spotted crimson
Triumphant - clear rose, spotted with carmine on the under lobes
Teneriffe - purplish violet, throat white and purple
Tina Forbes - bright crimson with white throat, veined and margined bronzy chocolate
Tom Page - crimson, suffused purple, large open throat, veined chocolate
Titian - white, shaded lilac, enormous flowers
Thomas M'Crorie - rosy lilac, large open throat, finely pencilled and margined chocolate
Trocadero - purplish crimson, white throat, beautifully streaked crimson
Victor Hugo - lilac, white throat, pencilled purple
Virginale - one of the finest whites
Waverley - rosy scarlet, white throat, pencilled and spotted cream
Walter Speed - clear purple, large, open pure white throat, slightly veined crimson
Walter Scott - rosy purple, white throat, heavily pencilled crimson
W.E. Gladstone - crimson, blotched chocolate
William Lumley - bright red, throat heavily pencilled chocolate
W.M.Baillie - bright scarlet, pure white throat
W.M.Whyte - purple, spotted and margined white
William Browne (1896) - scarlet shaded rose,
William Hough - purplish violet, white throat, veined crimson
William Park - rosy purple, pencilled chocolate
W.Wilson - rosy lilac, white throat, pencilled chocolate
William Totty (1896) - crimson scarlet, large open throat, veined crimson, enormous flowers
William Montgomery - violet purple, pure white throat, edged chocolate
W.Moorman (1896) - rosy purple, white throat, veined and maculated chocolate
Xavier Marmier (1896) - rosy violet, white throat, veined and blotched purple throat, veined chocolate
Scapin (1896) - clear violet with reddish purple

$\mathcal{H}$olders of $\mathcal{N}$ational $\mathcal{P}$enstemon $\mathcal{C}$ollections

KINGSTON MAURWARD GARDENS
Kingston Maurward
DORCHESTER
Dorset. DT2 8PY

CLIVE AND KATHY GANDLEY
The Old Custom House
Gatcombe Lane
GATCOMBE
Gloucester. GL15 4AU

PERSHORE COLLEGE OF
HORTICULTURE
PERSHORE
Worcester. WR10 3JP

M.C.SNOWDEN B.E.M.
The National Trust
Rowallane Garden
Saintfield
BALLYNAHINCH
County Down
Northen Ireland. BT24 7LH

LIST OF MAIN STOCKISTS

ASHWOOD NURSERIES
Greens Forge
Kings Winford
West Midlands. DY6 0AE

HARDY'S COTTAGE GARDEN
PLANTS
The Walled Garden
Laverstoke Park
Laverstoke
Whitchurch
Hants. RG28 7NT

HOPLEYS PLANTS LTD
High Street
Much Hadham
Herts. SG10 6BU

MRS COOPER
Glen Cerrig
East Lane
Everton
Lymington
Hants. SO41 0JL